Contemporary's

WORD POWER

Spelling and Vocabulary in Context

Advanced

1

McGraw Hill — Wright Group

Acknowledgments

Series Developer
Phil LeFaivre
      Cottage Communications
      Sandwich, Massachusetts

Series Reviewer
Joan Loncich
      Instructor, Adult Basic Education
      Barnstable Community Schools
      Hyannis, Massachusetts

Wright Group

ISBN: 0-8092-0838-5

Send all inquiries to:
Wright Group/McGraw-Hill
130 East Randolph Street, Suite 400
Chicago, Illinois 60601

Printed in the United States of America.

10 11 12 13 14 15 BAH 08 07 06 05

The **McGraw·Hill** Companies

Credits

Market Development Manager

Noreen Lopez

Editorial Development Director

Cynthia Krejcsi

Project Manager

Laurie Duncan

Interior Design and Production

PiperStudiosInc

Cover Design

Kristy Sheldon

Word Power
Table of Contents

To the Teacher

Goals of the Series

Word Power provides the mature learner with a systematic program of instruction for reading, writing, and spelling the words needed on the job, at home, and in the community. The vocabulary is arranged thematically at appropriate levels of difficulty and presented in meaningful contexts.

Key Features

1. Word Power *provides instruction at five levels of difficulty, so you can select the book that precisely fits your students' needs.*

   Each of the five *Word Power* books is keyed to a level of the *Tests of Adult Basic Education*, Forms 7 & 8. The *Introductory Level* correlates with Level L. *Word Power Intermediate 1* and *Intermediate 2* are tied to TABE levels E and M. *Word Power Advanced 1* and *Advanced 2* match levels D and A. The four upper-level books offer a pre-test to confirm appropriateness of level and to provide a comparison for post-test purposes.

2. *Words are presented in meaningful contexts. Students immediately see the importance of what they are studying and become motivated to complete the work successfully.*

   Units in the four upper-level books are keyed to one of six Comprehensive Adult Student Assessment System (CASAS) Life Skills Competencies: Consumer Economics, Health, Employment, Community Resources, Government and Law, and Learning to Learn.

3. *The skills of reading, writing, and spelling are synchronized to facilitate learning and build a portfolio of successful work.*

   Once students have analyzed the meaning and spelling of the words, they can apply what they have learned in a practical writing and proofreading exercise. A number of the letters, announcements, or similar realistic messages that students write can be mailed or kept in a portfolio of each student's work.

4. *Regular review tests in standardized testing formats allow you to monitor progress while familiarizing your students with the testing strategies they will find in typical GED exams and tests of adult basic skills.*

   Every four-lesson unit concludes with a two-page review test. It checks each student's progress in mastering the meaning and spelling of the words. The testing formats match those used by the TABE.

5. *The easy-to-use format and a Mini-Dictionary at the four upper levels empower students to take control of their learning and work with a high degree of independence.*

   Each lesson follows a sequence through four key stages of learning, described on page 8. Students can work independently and progress at their own rate.

6. *The important* Introductory *book provides basic instruction in the key phonetic principles and mechanics skills in a meaningful adult context.*

   Unlike most programs for mature learners, *Word Power* provides instruction in the basic principles of sounds and letters, and it accomplishes this through high-interest, mature content.

Using the Advanced 1 Book

Like all the books in this series, *Advanced 1* consists of twenty-four lessons. After each unit of four lessons, a review test is provided to check progress. Each lesson is divided into four parts. Each part brings to closure a coherent step in the learning process. Depending on your students and your instructional time block, one or more parts or an entire lesson might constitute a class session.

The reading level in this book has been carefully controlled. It matches the reading level of TABE Level D.

The Pre-test on pages 10 and 11 will provide assistance in evaluating how much your students know and placing them in the appropriate *Word Power* text. No single test, however, should serve as the sole guide to placement. Used in conjunction with other tests of reading and writing, as well as your own observations, this Pre-test can serve as a valuable resource. The test has a multiple-choice format. Random guessing will result in a number of correct answers, so it is wise to expect a high level of mastery before deciding to move students to the next level. In addition, the lessons in this text include many related language skills not covered in the Pre-test. A better strategy might be to allow students who do well on the Pre-test to progress through the lessons independently at an accelerated pace.

The Post-test on pages 144 and 145 can serve as a handy tool for checking progress. Both tests cover selected words in this text, so a comparison of scores will provide a gauge of each student's progress.

In addition to the Pre-test and Post-test, each text includes a Personal Word List page and a How to Use the Dictionary page. The Personal Word List page allows students to record words encountered outside the classroom. These words can be studied using the steps in How to Study a Word on page 9. They can also be shared and discussed with the class as a means of enhancing each lesson. This is usually best done as part of the writing and proofreading part of the lesson.

The instructions for completing each part are clearly stated and could be performed by many students with a high degree of independence. You may prefer to have students check their own work using the Answer Key on pages 167 through 172. They can record the number correct in the space provided at the bottom of most pages.

As you can see, *Word Power* is an effective and practical tool for addressing the needs of a wide variety of adult learners. We feel confident that *Word Power* will make a significant contribution to your vital work as a teacher.

Breaking Down a Lesson

Each lesson in *Word Power* progresses through the following stages of instruction:

(A) Check the Meaning

On these two pages, students read the words in the context of one or two essays related to the unit theme. Students are asked to infer the meanings of the words from the context and then choose the correct definitions in a multiple-choice format. These exercises, like most of the exercises in the lessons, lend themselves easily to both independent and cooperative learning.

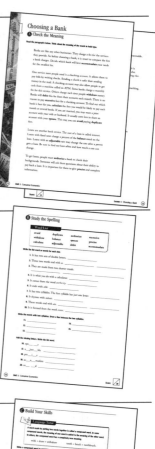

(B) Study the Spelling

This page contains a wide variety of exercises designed to focus attention on the letters and word parts that make up the spelling of each word. Emphasis is placed on noting coherent clusters of letters, tricky sound/letter combinations, and related and inflected forms of the words.

(C) Build Your Skills

Using one or more of the list words as a springboard, this part focuses attention on important language skills, such as recognizing homophones, inflectional endings, prefixes, suffixes, capitalization, and punctuation. Practice activities follow a concise statement of the rule and examples.

(D) Proofread and Write

The lessons conclude by having students apply what they have learned. First students proofread an example of writing related to the lesson theme. Then they correct the errors they find. This is followed by a structured writing assignment modeled on the format they have just proofread. Students proofread and correct their own work and make a final copy for their writing portfolios. Cooperative learning strategies can be employed by having students share a draft of their written work with a classmate and solicit his or her response before making the final copy.

How to Study a Word

Follow these steps for learning how to spell new words.

1 **Look** at the word.

- How many syllables does it have?
- Do you know what the word means?

2 **Say** the word aloud.

- What vowel sounds do you hear?
- What consonant sounds do you hear?

3 **Cover** the word.

- Can you see the word in your mind?
- What are the sounds and letters in the word?

4 **Write** the word.

- How is each sound spelled?
- Can you form the letters carefully?

5 **Check** the spelling.

- Did you spell the word correctly?

6 If you make a mistake, repeat the steps.

Pre-test

Part 1: Meaning

For each item below, fill in the letter next to the word or phrase that most nearly expresses the meaning of the first word.

> ### Sample
>
> hammer
>
> (A) part of the arm   (C) a type of vegetable
> ● a tool used for driving nails   (D) to mix thoroughly

1. diversity
- (A) foolish
- (B) complexity
- (C) shortness
- (D) variety

2. physician
- (A) person who cares for the ill
- (B) person who does magic tricks
- (C) person who teaches in a college
- (D) person who trains animals

3. inhibit
- (A) to hold back
- (B) to live in
- (C) to make larger
- (D) to forget

4. verify
- (A) to clean thoroughly
- (B) to remove from view
- (C) to prove true
- (D) to change shape

5. impartial
- (A) fair
- (B) small
- (C) rude
- (D) slow

6. stamina
- (A) appearance
- (B) property
- (C) strength
- (D) height and weight

7. device
- (A) a bad habit
- (B) a squeeze
- (C) a machine or gadget
- (D) something that separates in two

8. hygiene
- (A) a dog-like animal
- (B) someone who grants wishes
- (C) habits that promote good health
- (D) an active adult

9. adept
- (A) easily confused
- (B) to take as one's own
- (C) skillful
- (D) uncertain

10. spouse
- (A) a marriage partner
- (B) a religious leader
- (C) a business partner
- (D) a type of tree

Part 2: Spelling

For each item below, fill in the letter next to the correct spelling of the word.

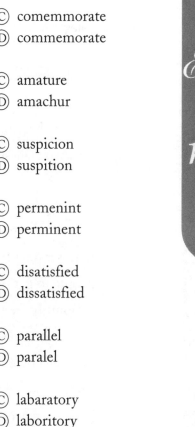

11. Ⓐ munisipal   Ⓒ municipal
    Ⓑ municiple   Ⓓ munisipul

12. Ⓐ associate   Ⓒ accosiate
    Ⓑ assosiate   Ⓓ assocaite

13. Ⓐ reside   Ⓒ razide
    Ⓑ raside   Ⓓ resied

14. Ⓐ bizness   Ⓒ busness
    Ⓑ buziness   Ⓓ business

15. Ⓐ privilige   Ⓒ privilije
    Ⓑ privilege   Ⓓ previlege

16. Ⓐ tendancy   Ⓒ tendency
    Ⓑ tendencie   Ⓓ tandancy

17. Ⓐ gaje   Ⓒ guage
    Ⓑ gaige   Ⓓ gauge

18. Ⓐ suceeding   Ⓒ succeding
    Ⓑ succeeding   Ⓓ sucieding

19. Ⓐ column   Ⓒ colum
    Ⓑ colunm   Ⓓ culumn

20. Ⓐ purjury   Ⓒ perjery
    Ⓑ perjury   Ⓓ perjurie

21. Ⓐ commemmorate Ⓒ comemmorate
    Ⓑ comemorate   Ⓓ commemorate

22. Ⓐ amateur   Ⓒ amature
    Ⓑ amatuer   Ⓓ amachur

23. Ⓐ suspishun   Ⓒ suspicion
    Ⓑ saspicion   Ⓓ suspition

24. Ⓐ permenent   Ⓒ permenint
    Ⓑ permanent   Ⓓ perminent

25. Ⓐ dissadisfied Ⓒ disatisfied
    Ⓑ disatasfied   Ⓓ dissatisfied

26. Ⓐ parralel   Ⓒ parallel
    Ⓑ paralell   Ⓓ paralel

27. Ⓐ labratory   Ⓒ labaratory
    Ⓑ laboratory   Ⓓ laboritory

28. Ⓐ guarantee   Ⓒ guarantie
    Ⓑ garauntee   Ⓓ gaurantee

29. Ⓐ receit   Ⓒ raceipt
    Ⓑ reciept   Ⓓ receipt

30. Ⓐ acomodate   Ⓒ accommodate
    Ⓑ accomodate   Ⓓ acommodate

Score ⬜/30

Choosing a Bank

Ⓐ Check the Meaning

Read the paragraphs below. Think about the meaning of the words in bold type.

Banks are like any other businesses. They charge a fee for the services they provide. So before choosing a bank, it is smart to compare the fees a bank charges. Decide which bank will best **accommodate** your needs for the smallest fee.

One service most people need is a checking account. Checking accounts let people pay bills by writing checks. Sending a check is safer than sending money in the mail. A checking account may also allow people to get cash from a machine called an ATM. Some banks charge a monthly fee for this service. Others charge each time people **withdraw** money. Banks will **debit** this fee from their accounts each month. There is no reason to pay **excessive** fees for a checking account. To find out which bank is best for you, **calculate** the fees you would be likely to pay each month at several banks. If you are married, you may want a joint account with your wife or husband. It usually costs less to share an account with your **spouse**. This way you can **avoid** paying **duplicate** fees.

A loan is another bank service. The cost of a loan is called interest. Loans with fixed interest rates charge a percent of the **balance** owed on the loan. Loans with an **adjustable** rate may change the rate after a person gets a loan. Be sure to find out how often and how much a rate can change.

To get loans, people must **authorize** a bank to check their backgrounds. Someone will ask them questions about their ability to pay back a loan. It is important for people to give **precise** and complete information.

Check the Meaning

Choose the correct meaning for the word in bold type. Fill in the circle next to the correct meaning.

1. When people **calculate** something, they
   - Ⓐ move it about.
   - Ⓑ use math to figure it out.
   - Ⓒ strengthen it.
   - Ⓓ write it carefully.

2. To **debit** is
   - Ⓐ to show in public for the first time.
   - Ⓑ to argue.
   - Ⓒ to subtract from.
   - Ⓓ to add to.

3. A **spouse** is
   - Ⓐ a marriage partner.
   - Ⓑ someone who works for a bank.
   - Ⓒ a business partner.
   - Ⓓ a type of tree.

4. Something that is **adjustable** is
   - Ⓐ fixed and immovable.
   - Ⓑ fair.
   - Ⓒ placed beside an object.
   - Ⓓ changeable.

5. When people **accommodate** a need, they
   - Ⓐ praise it.
   - Ⓑ make it go faster.
   - Ⓒ take care of it.
   - Ⓓ tell others about it.

6. The **balance** on a loan is
   - Ⓐ the amount that is still owed.
   - Ⓑ information given by the bank.
   - Ⓒ the time it takes to repay it.
   - Ⓓ a fee paid when someone asks for the loan.

7. An **excessive** cost is
   - Ⓐ highly desirable.
   - Ⓑ more than is usual or reasonable.
   - Ⓒ reasonable and fair.
   - Ⓓ small.

8. If something is a **duplicate**, it is
   - Ⓐ the same as something else.
   - Ⓑ the opposite of something else.
   - Ⓒ false and confusing.
   - Ⓓ easy to understand.

9. When people **withdraw** something, they
   - Ⓐ pay for it.
   - Ⓑ make it larger.
   - Ⓒ give it to someone.
   - Ⓓ take it out.

10. To **authorize** means
    - Ⓐ to write down.
    - Ⓑ to thank.
    - Ⓒ to give power to.
    - Ⓓ to give credit for.

11. If you **avoid** something, you
    - Ⓐ learn about it.
    - Ⓑ pay no attention to it.
    - Ⓒ keep away from it.
    - Ⓓ deny it.

12. **Precise** information is
    - Ⓐ without value.
    - Ⓑ not clear and correct.
    - Ⓒ less than needed.
    - Ⓓ exact.

B Study the Spelling

Word List

avoid	duplicate	authorize	excessive
withdraw	balance	spouse	precise
calculate	adjustable	debit	accommodate

Write the list word or words for each clue.

1. It has two sets of double letters. _____

2. These two words end with *se*. _____ _____

3. It is made from two shorter words. _____

4. It is what you do with a calculator. _____

5. It comes from the word *authority*. _____

6. It ends with the suffix *-able*. _____

7. It has two syllables. The first syllable has just one letter. _____

8. It rhymes with *talents*. _____

9. These words end with *ate*. _____

_____ _____

10. It is formed from the word *excess*. _____

Write the words with two syllables. Use a dot between the two syllables.

11. _____   **14.** _____

12. _____   **15.** _____

13. _____

Add the missing letters. Write the list word.

16. spo___ ___e _____

17. a___just___ble _____

18. pre___i___e _____

19. ac___o___modate _____

20. av___ ___d _____

Score: 20

C Build Your Skills

Language Tutor

A word made by putting two words together is called a compound word. In some compound words, the meaning of one word is added to the meaning of the other word. In others, the compound word has a completely new meaning.

with + draw = withdraw   tooth + brush = toothbrush

Write a compound word to complete each statement. The underlined words or letters will give you a clue.

1. I have a bad <u>ache</u> in my <u>head</u>. It is a bad _____.

2. She is <u>free</u> of all her <u>cares</u>. She is a _____ person.

3. Have you ever visited the <u>place</u> of your <u>birth</u>? It is always interesting to see your

   _____.

4. Sandra cut her <u>bare</u> <u>foot</u>. She was running _____ through the grass.

5. My thanks will be <u>lasting</u> for<u>ever</u>. It is _____.

6. I want to be a <u>person</u> who works in <u>sales</u>. I think I will enjoy being a

   _____.

7. This jelly was <u>made</u> at <u>home</u>. I love _____ jelly.

8. The <u>back</u> of the book is made of <u>paper</u>. A _____ book costs less.

9. I need someone to <u>cut</u> my <u>hair</u>. Where can I get a _____?

10. Juan is <u>worthy</u> of our <u>trust</u>. He is one of the most _____ people I know.

Add a word from the first column to a word from the second column. Write a compound word.

no	mate	11. _____
heart	head	12. _____
room	age	13. _____
fore	broken	14. _____
teen	where	15. _____

D Proofread and Write

Holly had some questions about the fees at her bank. She wrote this letter to her bank. Holly made four spelling mistakes. Cross out the misspelled words. Write the correct spellings above them.

399 South Avenue
Tampa, FL 33619
November 16, 1997

Customer Service Department
Wetlands National Bank
9001 Pine Street
Tampa, FL 33606

Dear Sir or Madam:

I do not understand the debbit you made to my account. There is a $2.00 charge for using the ATM. I did withdraw money. However, I thought I could aviod the charge if I had a balance of $100. This charge seems excesive. Please tell me how you calculate this charge.

I also see two monthly charges. I think the second charge is a duplicate of the first. My spouce and I opened an account together. I think there should be just one monthly charge.

Please let me know about these charges as soon as you can.

Sincerely,

Holly Silva

Holly Silva

Writing Portfolio

Write a letter to a bank. Use your own paper. Ask for information about the charges for a checking account. Use at least four list words.

Proofread your letter carefully and correct any mistakes. Then make a clean copy and put it in your writing portfolio.

Know What You Need

Ⓐ Check the Meaning

Read the paragraph below. Think about the meaning of the words in bold type.

Do you ever wonder why you bought certain things? Maybe you bought a dog collar, but you do not own a dog. If so, this should not **embarrass** you. Many people **accumulate** piles of junk because **clever** salespeople made them **crave** something they really did not need. One way they do this is by giving away coupons that buyers can **redeem** for dollars off the usual price. Another is to claim there is a **surplus** of certain items. Therefore, they must sell them at a very low price. It is hard to turn down a good deal. A good buy on something is a good buy only if it is for something you need. Of course, if you buy a dog collar, a salesperson might come back later to sell you the dog.

Choose the correct meaning for the word in bold type. Fill in the circle next to the correct meaning.

1. When people have a **surplus**, they have
Ⓐ just enough to get by.
Ⓑ more than they need.
Ⓒ none at all.
Ⓓ something costing very little.

2. A **clever** person is
Ⓐ unusually strong.
Ⓑ well educated.
Ⓒ outspoken.
Ⓓ bright and creative.

3. When people **redeem** a coupon, they
Ⓐ throw it away.
Ⓑ exchange it for something.
Ⓒ increase its value.
Ⓓ make it worthless.

4. To **accumulate** is
Ⓐ to join together.
Ⓑ to collect.
Ⓒ to destroy.
Ⓓ to reduce in size.

5. When people **embarrass** someone, they
Ⓐ hold a person gently.
Ⓑ explain something to a person.
Ⓒ make a person feel silly or uncomfortable.
Ⓓ express anger toward a person.

6. When people **crave** something, they
Ⓐ strongly dislike it.
Ⓑ divide it into parts.
Ⓒ use it up.
Ⓓ have a powerful desire for it.

Check the Meaning

Read the paragraph below. Think about the meaning of the words in bold type.

We might as well face it: people are lazy. Most homes give **ample** proof of this fact. We have electric can openers. The **fatigue** of getting up to change TV channels is just too much. Our TVs now have **remote** controls. There is a gimmick to fit every need we can think of. However, each new gimmick brings with it the chance that it won't work. A VCR with an **improper** hookup will not work. Be sure to choose things carefully before you buy. Look for items that are well made, not things that have lots of gimmicks but are poorly made. Then take care of the things you buy. Most stores will not repair things that are broken due to the owner's **negligence**. Getting the most from the things that make life easy requires **patience**. Read the directions for use carefully. Know how to take care of an object.

Choose the correct meaning for the word in bold type. Fill in the circle next to the correct meaning.

7. If something is **remote**, it is
- (A) dangerous.
- (B) far away.
- (C) worth a great deal of money.
- (D) difficult to use.

8. Someone suffering from **fatigue** is
- (A) very tired.
- (B) poorly dressed.
- (C) unable to read.
- (D) overweight.

9. An **improper** hookup
- (A) has been done by an expert.
- (B) has been done incorrectly.
- (C) is one that works.
- (D) is one that is unimportant.

10. When people have an **ample** amount of something, they have
- (A) a very tiny amount.
- (B) less than is needed.
- (C) none at all.
- (D) a very large quantity.

11. **Patience** is
- (A) the ability to stay calm for a long period of time.
- (B) a group of sick people.
- (C) the ability to do things quickly.
- (D) having the ability to speak several languages.

12. Someone guilty of **negligence**
- (A) eats too much.
- (B) lacks common sense.
- (C) is not careful about what he does.
- (D) is rude to others.

B Study the Spelling

Word List

embarrass	negligence	ample	redeem	remote	fatigue
accumulate	improper	clever	surplus	patience	crave

Write the list word or words for each clue.

1. It ends with a silent *ue*. _____

2. They end with a vowel, consonant, and *e*. _____

   _____   _____

3. They end with *ence*. _____   _____

4. They end with *er*. _____   _____

5. It has two pairs of double consonants. _____

6. The word *plus* is part of its spelling. _____

7. This two-syllable word has a double vowel in its spelling.

   _____

8. This two-syllable word begins with a vowel. _____

9. It is made up of the word *proper* and a prefix. _____

10. It has four syllables and a double consonant in its spelling.

    _____

Write *accumulate*, *negligence*, and *embarrass*. Use dots between the syllables.

11. _____   13. _____

12. _____

One word in each group is misspelled. Circle the misspelled word. Write it correctly.

14. fatique   accumulate   clever   _____

15. negligence   patiance   improper   _____

16. surplus   crave   redeam   _____

17. ampel   surplus   remote   _____

18. clever   embarass   accumulate   _____

© Build Your Skills

Language Tutor

A prefix is added to the beginning of a word. It changes the meaning of the word. The *im-* and *in-* prefixes add "not" to the meaning of a word. The *im-* prefix is used with words beginning with *p* or *m*.

im- + proper = improper, not proper
in- + complete = incomplete, not complete

Add the prefix to the word. Write a new word.

1. in- + sincere = _____

2. im- + mature = _____

3. in- + visible = _____

4. im- + possible = _____

5. im- + polite = _____

6. in- + dependent = _____

Complete the second sentence by adding a prefix to the underlined word in the first sentence. Write the second sentence.

7. The woman lost her <u>patience</u>. Her _____ was noticed by everyone.

_____

8. That clock cannot be <u>accurate</u>. We will be late for work if I have the _____ time.

_____

9. This is not a <u>direct</u> road to town. It takes an _____ route.

_____

10. The filter was used to make the water <u>pure</u>. It removes the _____ parts.

_____

Score: 10

Ⓓ Proofread and Write

Here are some rules for getting good buys. There are four spelling mistakes in the rules. Cross out the misspelled words. Write the correct spellings above them.

1. Have patience. Wait for the right item at the right price.

2. A clever shopper will not redeme coupons for things not needed.

3. Do not acumulate a surplus of items that will not keep.

4. A good price is no bargain if you must travel to some remote place to get it.

5. Be sure the clerk rings up the right amount. Correcting a mistake should not embarass you.

6. Report any improper or misleading ads to the manager. Such negligance should not be allowed.

Make a list of rules for smart shopping. Use at least four list words.

_____

_____

_____

_____

_____

_____

_____

_____

Writing Portfolio

Proofread your list carefully and correct any mistakes. Then make a clean copy and put it in your writing portfolio.

Getting Your Money's Worth

Ⓐ Check the Meaning

Read the paragraphs below. Think about the meaning of the words in bold type.

As the saying goes, "The customer is king." You, the customer, have a right to the **maximum** value for the dollars you spend. Sometimes getting your money's worth means taking certain **precautions**. The first is always to check closely the condition of an item you plan to buy. A **deficiency** may not be **obvious** to the eye, however. A toaster or can opener may look fine, but at home you may find that it does not work. Most stores will replace any item that is not **satisfactory**. In addition, the maker of the item will usually **guarantee** that it works properly. Both the store and maker will expect you to have the **receipt**. This will show when and where you bought the item. It also gives the price you paid. So the second precaution is to keep the receipt.

A guarantee may mean many things. Do not **accept vague** promises to correct any problems. A guarantee should always be in writing. A smart shopper reads it closely and makes an **inquiry** about any part that is not clear. This is the third important precaution. Some guarantees require that you mail in information about yourself and where you bought the item.

Finally, if the store or the maker of the item doesn't take care of a problem for you, know where to go for help. Most cities and states have offices that protect buyers. Anyone who tries to **exploit** buyers or fails to **honor** a guarantee should be reported. Most honest businesses will do anything needed to make a customer happy. The smart shopper, however, must be prepared for the few that do not.

Check the Meaning

Choose the correct meaning for the word in bold type. Fill in the circle next to the correct meaning.

1. A **vague** promise is
   - (A) mysterious.
   - (B) unclear.
   - (C) simple.
   - (D) unusual.

2. If something is **obvious**, it is
   - (A) hidden.
   - (B) dangerous.
   - (C) difficult to understand.
   - (D) easily seen.

3. A **receipt** is
   - (A) a recent event.
   - (B) written proof that you have received something.
   - (C) a promise to pay an amount of money.
   - (D) the maker of an item sold in stores.

4. The **maximum** amount is
   - (A) the most possible.
   - (B) the least possible.
   - (C) any amount agreed to by two people.
   - (D) less than desired.

5. A **deficiency** is
   - (A) something done quickly.
   - (B) an outstanding feature.
   - (C) a defect or fault.
   - (D) a defeated army.

6. If people **exploit** you, they
   - (A) take selfish advantage of you.
   - (B) lie about you.
   - (C) entertain you.
   - (D) explain something to you.

7. When people **honor** a promise, they
   - (A) deny it.
   - (B) tell everyone about it.
   - (C) respect or stand by it.
   - (D) change it.

8. To **accept** something is to
   - (A) replace it.
   - (B) take or receive it.
   - (C) remove it.
   - (D) require it.

9. A **precaution** is
   - (A) a step taken to avoid a problem.
   - (B) a dangerous situation.
   - (C) the high point in an area.
   - (D) anything that breaks a law.

10. A **guarantee** is
    - (A) a musical instrument.
    - (B) someone who guards a safe.
    - (C) a machine used in woodworking shops.
    - (D) a promise that something will work.

11. If an item is **satisfactory**, it
    - (A) often breaks.
    - (B) pleases its owner.
    - (C) has been made in a factory.
    - (D) cannot be replaced.

12. An **inquiry** is a
    - (A) question.
    - (B) funny story.
    - (C) loud noise.
    - (D) confusing message.

B Study the Spelling

Word List

deficiency	accept	exploit	vague	guarantee	satisfactory
maximum	receipt	obvious	honor	inquiry	precaution

Write the list word for each clue.

1. It is made from the word *satisfy*. _____

2. It is made from the word *deficient*. _____

3. It is made from the word *inquire*. _____

4. It begins with a prefix that means "before." _____

5. It has one syllable and ends with two silent vowels. _____

6. It ends with a double vowel. _____

7. It has two syllables and a double consonant. _____

8. There is an *ei* and a silent *p* in its spelling. _____

9. It begins with a silent consonant. _____

10. It has two syllables and rhymes with *Detroit*. _____

Write *obvious*, *maximum*, and *inquiry*. Use dots between the syllables.

11. _____   **13.** _____

12. _____

One word in each group is misspelled. Circle the misspelled word. Write it correctly.

14. honor   receipt   vauge   _____

15. deficency   obvious   accept   _____

16. satisfactory precaution   inquery   _____

17. exploit   guarantee   maxamum   _____

Circle the list word within each of these words. Write the list word.

18. unsatisfactory _____

19. acceptable _____

20. dishonor _____

C Build Your Skills

Words with similar sounds and spellings are often confused. The underlined words in each pair of sentences have similar sounds and spellings. Their meanings, however, are quite different.

Juanita will <u>accept</u> the prize. Everyone came <u>except</u> Ray.

I ordered pie for <u>dessert</u>. There is little water in the <u>desert</u>.

I was <u>already</u> dressed when he called. We are <u>all ready</u> to go.

They must <u>choose</u> a new manger soon. Last year they <u>chose</u> Ms. Lum.

Grab the <u>loose</u> end of the rope. We must not <u>lose</u> this game.

Write the sentences. Add the correct word from the parentheses.

1. I cannot _____ any more work. (accept; except)

_____

2. We will _____ a winner by Sunday. (choose; chose)

_____

3. It took six hours to drive through the _____. (dessert; desert)

_____

4. When I arrived, she was _____ there. (already; all ready)

_____

5. Try not to _____ the money I gave you. (loose; lose)

_____

6. A _____ wire might cause a fire. (loose; lose)

_____

7. Who _____ this awful movie? (choose; chose)

_____

8. I am too full to eat any _____. (dessert; desert)

_____

D Proofread and Write

The city sent the following rules for buyers to all homes in the city. The rules have five spelling mistakes. They also used the wrong word in a sentence. Cross out the misspelled words and the incorrect word. Write the correct spellings above them.

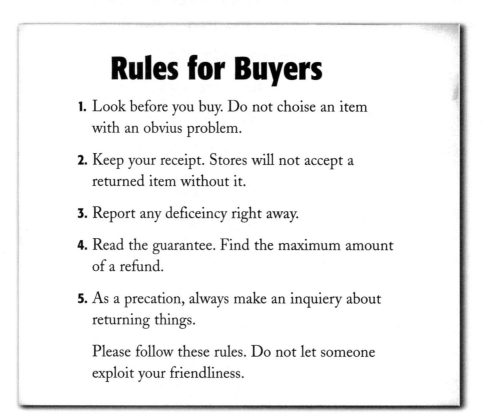

Rules for Buyers

1. Look before you buy. Do not choise an item with an obvius problem.

2. Keep your receipt. Stores will not accept a returned item without it.

3. Report any deficeincy right away.

4. Read the guarantee. Find the maximum amount of a refund.

5. As a precation, always make an inquiery about returning things.

   Please follow these rules. Do not let someone exploit your friendliness.

Write your own set of rules for being a smart buyer. Use at least four list words.

_____

_____

_____

_____

_____

_____

Writing Portfolio

Proofread your rules carefully and correct any mistakes. Then make a clean copy and put it in your writing portfolio.

Eat Smart!

Ⓐ Check the Meaning

Read the paragraph below. Think about the meaning of the words in bold type.

Today, a trip to the grocery store presents some difficult choices. Colorful advertising and a huge **assortment** of sale items **urge** people to buy one thing. Coupons and clever packages tempt them to buy other things. What is one to do? When grocery shopping, make these two things your **priorities**: good **nutrition** and a fair price. The cookie **aisle** may be very inviting, but a bag of carrots or apples from the produce section is cheaper and better for you. One way to avoid temptation is to plan several healthy meals. Then make a list of things you need to make those meals. When you get to the store, buy only those items. It makes sense to **investigate** sale items. However, do not buy something just because it is cheap or neatly wrapped. Always stick to your meal plans. There is one other smart rule for grocery shopping: Never go to the store when you are hungry.

Choose the correct meaning for the word in bold type. Fill in the circle next to the correct meaning.

1. **Nutrition** has to do with
   - Ⓐ shopping for sales.
   - Ⓑ the effect of food on health.
   - Ⓒ borrowing money.
   - Ⓓ exercise.

2. To **investigate** means to
   - Ⓐ give money to.
   - Ⓑ supply with water.
   - Ⓒ look into closely.
   - Ⓓ erase.

3. **Priorities** are
   - Ⓐ a type of breakfast food.
   - Ⓑ the important things.
   - Ⓒ a set of small rooms.
   - Ⓓ people playing a game.

4. An **aisle** is
   - Ⓐ a passageway between rows.
   - Ⓑ land surrounded by water.
   - Ⓒ a counter or shelf.
   - Ⓓ something that helps you see.

5. An **assortment** is
   - Ⓐ a lively new dance.
   - Ⓑ a photograph or picture.
   - Ⓒ an advertisement.
   - Ⓓ a group to choose from.

6. To **urge** is
   - Ⓐ to ridicule.
   - Ⓑ to report.
   - Ⓒ to trick.
   - Ⓓ to encourage.

Check the Meaning

Read the paragraph below. Think about the meaning of the words in bold type.

Do you panic when it is time to prepare dinner? Does the idea of another frozen dinner make you lose your **appetite**? The sight of limp vegetables and warmed-over meat on cardboard does not make one's mouth water. Soggy **texture** and **artificial** flavor are a high price to pay for **convenience**. However, long hours at your job may not leave much time for fancy meals. It takes practice and planning to create an **appealing** yet healthy dinner night after night. Here are some helpful hints. Make several dishes on the weekend that you can heat up after work. Chop vegetables and other things when you have time. Measure out the things you need for dinner in the morning. Then they will be ready to use when you get home. In a short time you will cook with **confidence**. You may even look forward to coming home to dinner.

Choose the correct meaning for the word in bold type. Fill in the circle next to the correct meaning.

7. The **texture** of something is its
- Ⓐ feel and appearance.
- Ⓑ color.
- Ⓒ price.
- Ⓓ ability to soak up water.

8. If people do things with **confidence**, they are
- Ⓐ breaking the law.
- Ⓑ doing them alone.
- Ⓒ sure they can do it.
- Ⓓ doing them slowly.

9. Your **appetite** is your
- Ⓐ ability to lift heavy things.
- Ⓑ intelligence.
- Ⓒ desire for food.
- Ⓓ love for the outdoors.

10. An **appealing** meal is one that
- Ⓐ costs a great deal of money.
- Ⓑ is pleasing to look at.
- Ⓒ is made at home.
- Ⓓ is overcooked.

11. If something is **artificial**, it is
- Ⓐ approved by an official.
- Ⓑ artistic.
- Ⓒ very desirable.
- Ⓓ not real or true.

12. A **convenience** is
- Ⓐ a type of car.
- Ⓑ the opposite of something else.
- Ⓒ a discussion between two people.
- Ⓓ something that is easy and comfortable.

Score: 12

B Study the Spelling

Word List

urge	confidence	texture	artificial	priorities	assortment
aisle	convenience	appetite	appealing	nutrition	investigate

Write the list word or words for each clue.

1. It is made from the word *convenient*. _____

2. It is the plural of *priority*. _____

3. It sounds like *I'll* and *isle*, but it has a different meaning and spelling.

_____

4. They end with *ence*. _____ _____

5. They each have a double consonant in their spelling.

_____ _____

_____

6. It begins like *artist* and ends like *official*. _____

7. They have just one syllable. _____

_____

8. It contains the word *text*. _____

Add the missing syllable. Write the list word.

9. inves_____gate _____

10. nutri_____ _____

11. ap_____tite _____

12. ap_____ing _____

One word in each group is misspelled. Circle the misspelled word. Write it correctly.

13. nutrishun   aisle   convenience   _____

14. appealing   texchur   artificial   _____

15. urje   confidence   assortment   _____

Score: ___/15

Lesson 4: Eat Smart!   **29**

© Build Your Skills

Language Tutor

The final *y* in a word is usually changed to *i* before adding an ending.

priority + -es = priorities   marry + -ed = married
heavy + -ly = heavily   cloudy + -ness = cloudiness
happy + -est = happiest   bounty + -ful = bountiful

Add the endings to these words. Write the word.

1. busy + -er = _____

2. heavy + -est = _____

3. dizzy + -ness = _____

4. city + -es = _____

5. mercy + -ful = _____

Write these sentences. Add the word and ending in parentheses to make the missing word.

6. I _____ for a job at the new store. (apply + -ed)

_____

7. The workers were _____ of the new hours. (notify + -ed)

_____

8. A meeting was _____ called. (hasty + -ly)

_____

9. Monday was the _____ day of the week. (windy + -est)

_____

10. Apples are _____ this time of year. (plenty + -ful)

_____

11. Nothing can change the _____ I feel. (happy + -ness)

_____

12. We sent her a bouquet of _____. (lily + -es)

_____

Score: 12

Ⓓ Proofread and Write

The manager of a cafeteria left these instructions for her staff. She made four spelling mistakes. Cross out the misspelled words. Write the correct spellings above them.

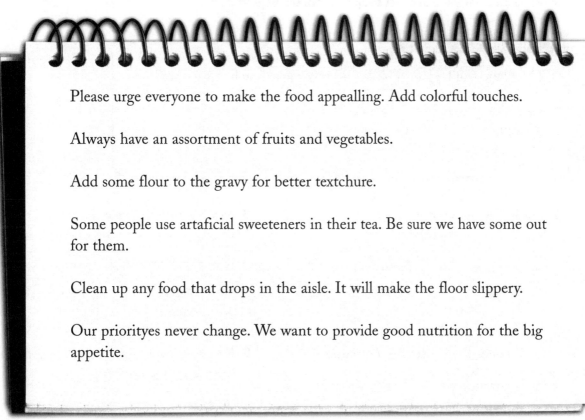

Please urge everyone to make the food appealling. Add colorful touches.

Always have an assortment of fruits and vegetables.

Add some flour to the gravy for better textchure.

Some people use artaficial sweeteners in their tea. Be sure we have some out for them.

Clean up any food that drops in the aisle. It will make the floor slippery.

Our priorityes never change. We want to provide good nutrition for the big appetite.

Write instructions for people using your kitchen. Use at least four list words.

_____

_____

_____

_____

_____

_____

_____

Writing Portfolio

Proofread your instructions carefully and correct any mistakes. Then make a clean copy and put it in your writing portfolio.

Unit 1 Review

Finish the Meaning

Fill in the circle next to the word that best completes each sentence.

Sample

The plane will be late. The _____ was caused by bad weather.

- ● delay
- Ⓑ rain
- Ⓒ worry
- Ⓓ angry

1. Fill in the name of your _____ or another close relative.

   Ⓐ surplus   Ⓒ aisle
   Ⓑ spouse   Ⓓ priorities

2. Try to help people in need, but do not let anyone _____ your good nature.

   Ⓐ guarantee   Ⓒ exploit
   Ⓑ embarrass   Ⓓ debit

3. Good health depends on good _____.

   Ⓐ balance   Ⓒ priorities
   Ⓑ nutrition   Ⓓ honor

4. The directions were so _____ that Dara could not find the house.

   Ⓐ vague   Ⓒ clever
   Ⓑ obvious   Ⓓ ample

5. Silly mistakes are usually caused by _____.

   Ⓐ precautions   Ⓒ negligence
   Ⓑ preparation   Ⓓ nutrition

6. Most banks charge a monthly fee. Often they _____ that amount from your account.

   Ⓐ investigate   Ⓒ debit
   Ⓑ crave   Ⓓ urge

7. Ken runs every day because health and fitness are his top _____.

   Ⓐ balances   Ⓒ receipts
   Ⓑ priorities   Ⓓ inquiries

8. A vitamin _____ can lead to serious illness.

   Ⓐ maximum   Ⓒ convenience
   Ⓑ assortment   Ⓓ deficiency

9. The interest on the loan will increase next month because it has a(n) _____ rate.

   Ⓐ adjustable   Ⓒ duplicate
   Ⓑ obvious   Ⓓ improper

10. Lee was too tired to drive home. She had never felt such _____ before.

    Ⓐ honor   Ⓒ fatigue
    Ⓑ negligence   Ⓓ inquiry

GO ON

Check the Spelling

Fill in the circle next to the word that is spelled correctly and best completes each sentence.

11. Put your money in a savings account. There it will _____ interest.

    (A) acumulate   (C) accumulait

    (B) accumulate   (D) acummulate

12. You must have a _____ to return an item to a store.

    (A) receept   (C) receipt

    (B) receit   (D) raceipt

13. Make a budget to avoid spending an _____ amount at the grocery store.

    (A) excessive   (C) excesive

    (B) exccesive   (D) eksessive

14. Even after a big meal, the chocolate cake was too _____ to resist.

    (A) appealling   (C) apieliing

    (B) apeeling   (D) appealing

15. Any plan should be flexible enough to _____ necessary changes.

    (A) acommodate   (C) acomodate

    (B) accomodate   (D) accommodate

16. The sofa had a rough, uncomfortable _____. No one wanted to sit on it.

    (A) texure   (C) texture

    (B) teksture   (D) textur

17. Teaching someone to drive takes great _____.

    (A) patence   (C) pashence

    (B) pateince   (D) patience

18. Always give _____ answers to a doctor's questions.

    (A) precise   (C) presise

    (B) pracise   (D) precice

19. The teacher would _____ only my very best work.

    (A) accept   (C) acept

    (B) aceppt   (D) aksept

20. Do not _____ coupons for things you do not need.

    (A) rediem   (C) redeam

    (B) redeem   (D) radeem

STOP

Score: _____ / 20

Are You Covered?

Ⓐ Check the Meaning

Read the paragraphs below. Think about the meaning of the words in bold type.

Given the high cost of medical care today, **insurance** is an important way to protect you and your family. Whether your employer provides insurance or you buy it from an insurance company, you should know what your plan covers. Here are five things to consider:

1. Do you risk the **cancellation** of your insurance if you have a serious illness? Insurance is for your protection. If your insurance can be dropped just when you need it, you are not protected.

2. Does your insurance cover the **expense** of **laboratory** tests? Blood tests and similar work can be quite costly. A good insurance plan will cover them.

3. If you are **dissatisfied** with one doctor or clinic, can you go to another? Some plans **restrict** your ability to choose a doctor.

4. Some plans do not cover such things as drug **abuse** counseling or an unusual medical **technique**, such as a heart transplant. Know ahead of time what is covered.

5. Find out if your plan limits the days you may stay in a hospital. Some plans may force you to leave the hospital before you can fully **recuperate** from an operation or illness. If so, talk to your doctor to be sure this will not be a problem.

Finally, ask for an **itemized** list of any expenses. Discuss any charges that seem too high. Also, all personal and medical information should be kept **confidential**. No one except the proper medical **personnel** should see your files.

Check the Meaning

Choose the correct meaning for the word in bold type. Fill in the circle next to the correct meaning.

1. **Personnel** are
   - (A) types of serious illnesses.
   - (B) the important parts of a report.
   - (C) workers in an organization.
   - (D) machines used in an office.

2. When people are **dissatisfied** with something, they
   - (A) value it highly.
   - (B) change it often.
   - (C) share it with others.
   - (D) are not happy with it.

3. **Insurance** is
   - (A) a system for buying protection from loss.
   - (B) something that is taught, such as a lesson.
   - (C) something that makes music.
   - (D) a bill sent by a hospital.

4. People who **restrict** something
   - (A) pay no attention to it.
   - (B) turn it over.
   - (C) limit it.
   - (D) show it to everyone.

5. A **technique** is a
   - (A) way of doing something.
   - (B) person's mood or state of mind.
   - (C) serious mistake.
   - (D) hidden meaning.

6. A **cancellation** is
   - (A) something that has been covered.
   - (B) the act of ending something.
   - (C) a type of boat.
   - (D) the act of improving something.

7. **Confidential** information is
   - (A) unbelievable.
   - (B) false.
   - (C) open to everyone.
   - (D) personal or secret.

8. An **expense** is
   - (A) a cost.
   - (B) an excuse.
   - (C) a free service.
   - (D) a false statement.

9. If you **recuperate** from something, you
   - (A) forget it.
   - (B) recover from it.
   - (C) pay for it.
   - (A) borrow it.

10. A **laboratory** is a
    - (A) place to wash your hands.
    - (B) room where labor unions meet.
    - (C) place where tests and experiments are done.
    - (D) storeroom.

11. An **itemized** list
    - (A) includes every part or detail.
    - (B) is written in a foreign language.
    - (C) is in alphabetical order.
    - (D) is unreadable.

12. An **abuse** is
    - (A) a form of exercise.
    - (B) any important goal.
    - (C) a harmful or cruel habit.
    - (D) something found in great amounts.

Score: /12

B Study the Spelling

Word List

restrict	itemized	personnel	confidential
cancellation	laboratory	abuse	technique
recuperate	dissatisfied	expense	insurance

Write the list word that comes from each of these words.

1. item _____

2. person _____

3. labor _____

4. dissatisfy _____

5. insure _____

6. confidence _____

Write the list word or words for each clue.

7. It ends with a silent *ue*. _____

8. It has two syllables. The first syllable has just one letter.

_____

9. They begin with the *re-* prefix.

_____   _____

10. They end with *se*. _____   _____

11. They have a double consonant in their spelling.

_____   _____   _____

12. There are two *a*'s and two *o*'s in its spelling. _____

Add an ending to make a list word. Write the list word.

13. item_____   _____

14. cancel_____   _____

Add a beginning to make a list word. Write the list word.

15. _____pense   _____

16. _____nique   _____

C Build Your Skills

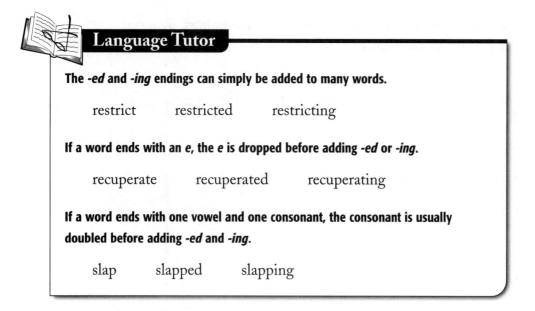

Language Tutor

The *-ed* and *-ing* endings can simply be added to many words.

    restrict   restricted   restricting

If a word ends with an *e*, the *e* is dropped before adding *-ed* or *-ing*.

    recuperate   recuperated   recuperating

If a word ends with one vowel and one consonant, the consonant is usually doubled before adding *-ed* and *-ing*.

    slap   slapped   slapping

Add *-ed* or *-ing* to these words.

1. stop + -ed = _____

2. explain + -ing = _____

3. confide + -ed = _____

4. insure + -ing = _____

5. please + -ed = _____

6. chop + -ing = _____

Write each sentence. Add *-ed* or *-ing* to the underlined word.

7. This room is <u>restrict</u> to members of the staff. Only they may enter.

_____

8. The clerk is <u>itemize</u> our bill.

_____

9. The rabbit went <u>hop</u> through the yard.

_____

10. I am <u>hope</u> to see her at the game.

_____

D Proofread and Write

Rolanda must go to the hospital for tests. She made a list of questions she wanted to ask when she was admitted. Rolanda made four spelling mistakes. Cross out the misspelled words. Write the correct spellings above them.

Questions

- Which hospital personel will do these tests?

- Is there a TV in my room? If so, is this an additional expense?

- Do you restrict the hours when I may have visitors?

- Are meetings with my doctor confadential?

- What technick is used to get a blood sample?

- Will I have the test results from the laboratory before I leave?

- If my doctor is disatisfied with the results, can she reorder the tests?

- How long does it usually take to recuperate after I am released?

Writing Portfolio

Make a list of questions you would like to ask of a hospital you use. Use your own paper. Use at least four list words.

Proofread your questions carefully and correct any mistakes. Then make a clean copy and put it in your writing portfolio.

See Your Doctor

A Check the Meaning

Read the paragraph below. Think about the meaning of the words in bold type.

One of the most important choices you make is your choice of a **physician**. Do not wait until you suffer an **injury** or illness to make this choice. It is much better to see a doctor before you need one. This way the doctor or an **assistant** can record your medical history. You will be asked if you are taking any **medicines**. Someone will probably check your blood **pressure**. This measures the force of the blood on the walls of your blood vessels. Any history of illness or **disease** will also go into your file. These facts will help a doctor decide how to treat you for an illness or injury. Having this and other information about you on hand could save valuable time in an emergency.

Choose the correct meaning for the word in bold type. Fill in the circle next to the correct meaning.

1. **Medicine** is
   - (A) something taken to cure an illness.
   - (B) a person training to be a doctor.
   - (C) useful information.
   - (D) a dish served with dinner.

2. A **disease** is a
   - (A) comfortable position.
   - (B) long delay.
   - (C) sickness.
   - (D) display of courage.

3. When people put **pressure** on something, they
   - (A) write on it.
   - (B) press on it.
   - (C) remove it forcefully.
   - (D) examine it.

4. Another word for **physician** is
   - (A) magician.
   - (B) doctor.
   - (C) professor.
   - (D) priest.

5. Your **assistant** is someone who
   - (A) pays you for your work.
   - (B) gives out assignments.
   - (C) helps you do something.
   - (D) wears a uniform.

6. If someone has an **injury**, he or she
   - (A) has been harmed or hurt.
   - (B) is unable to speak clearly.
   - (C) dresses in plain clothes.
   - (D) is skillful with tools.

Check the Meaning

Read the paragraph below. Think about the meaning of the words in bold type.

Some jobs, like those of cooks and hospital aides, require people to pass regular **physical** examinations. There are good reasons for such checkups for these workers. However, an annual physical is a good idea for everyone. Going to a doctor when one feels healthy may not seem to make sense. Yet a physical is usually quite simple. Here is what you might expect: The doctor will listen to your heart and lungs as you **breathe** deeply. Sometimes a test of your **stamina** will also be given. If so, the doctor will **monitor** your heart and blood pressure while you walk or run. You will probably be asked to describe any recent problems such as **headaches** or any difficulty with sleeping, hearing, or seeing. Finally, your **signature** may be needed on a paper. This will give your doctor the right to share his or her report with another doctor or with your employer.

Choose the correct meaning for the word in bold type. Fill in the circle next to the correct meaning.

7. When people **monitor** something, they
- Ⓐ pay little attention to it.
- Ⓑ watch it closely.
- Ⓒ divide it into parts.
- Ⓓ make copies of it.

8. A **physical** examination is an examination
- Ⓐ done at your job or school.
- Ⓑ using x-rays and other equipment.
- Ⓒ of your body and how it works.
- Ⓓ of your mental ability.

9. When you **breathe**, you
- Ⓐ strike your breast several times.
- Ⓑ take air into your lungs.
- Ⓒ eat a large meal.
- Ⓓ move your arms and legs.

10. A **headache** is
- Ⓐ a curved area above a door.
- Ⓑ a place shaded by trees.
- Ⓒ any work that requires a lot of thought.
- Ⓓ a pain in the area of the head.

11. A person's **stamina** is his or her
- Ⓐ appearance.
- Ⓑ property.
- Ⓒ strength.
- Ⓓ height and weight.

12. Your **signature** is
- Ⓐ your name as you write it.
- Ⓑ a mixture of some kind.
- Ⓒ your name as you say it.
- Ⓓ a number given to you by the government.

Score: 12

B Study the Spelling

Word List

physical	signature	stamina	medicine	disease	injury
monitor	breathe	headache	pressure	physician	assistant

Write the list word or words for each clue.

1. They begin with *phy*. _____ _____

2. It is made up of two smaller words. _____

3. It rhymes with *seethe*. _____

4. They have a double *s* in their spelling.

_____ _____

5. It has three syllables and six letters. _____

6. It begins like *sign* and ends like *literature*. _____

7. The word *ease* is part of its spelling. _____

8. It has two *o*'s. _____

Write *medicine*, *stamina*, *disease*, and *signature*. Use dots between the syllables.

9. _____ **11.** _____

10. _____ **12.** _____

Add the missing letters. Write a list word.

13. bre___th___ _____

14. pres___ ___re _____

15. physi___ ___an _____

One word in each group is misspelled. Circle the misspelled word. Write it correctly.

16. stamina   headach   injury   _____

17. physical   physician   assistent   _____

18. medacine   monitor   pressure   _____

C Build Your Skills

Language Tutor

An abbreviation is a short way of writing one or more words. Often, but not always, it is made from the letters in the word or words.

M.D.	Doctor of Medicine	IRS	Internal Revenue Service
D.V.M.	Doctor of Veterinary Medicine	IBM	International Business Machines

Match the abbreviation with the word or words it stands for. Write the letter for the correct word or words next to its abbreviation.

_____ **1.** mpg   **a.** Federal Bureau of Investigation

_____ **2.** CD   **b.** post meridiem, (after noon)

_____ **3.** inc.   **c.** district attorney

_____ **4.** D.A.   **d.** compact disc

_____ **5.** RAM   **e.** miles per gallon

_____ **6.** FBI   **f.** incorporated

_____ **7.** P.M.   **g.** random access memory

Write these sentences. Replace the underlined word or words with an abbreviation.

8. Our manager has a <u>Master of Business Administration</u> degree from Yale University.

_____

_____

9. I swim every day at the <u>Young Men's Christian Association</u> pool.

_____

_____

10. The star of the baseball team was credited with a <u>run batted in</u>.

_____

_____

Ⓓ Proofread and Write

Teresa's son brought this note from the school nurse. The nurse made four spelling mistakes.
Cross out the misspelled words. Write the correct spellings above them.

Dear Ms. Lopez:

Richie seems to have less stamana than others in
his class. He finds it hard to breath after running or playing.
He also tells me he has had a headache most of the day.

He seemed fine when he had his physical exam last
week. He may have caught a cold or the flu. I suggest you
moniter his condition and see a physician if he does not
improve. If he needs to take a medicine, it may make him
sleepy. To avoid injery perhaps you should keep him at home.

School rules make it necessary to have a doctor's
signature if Richie is out of school for more than three days.
If you see a doctor, be sure he signs a note for school.

Sincerely,

Anne Silva

Anne Silva, R. N.

School Nurse

Writing Portfolio

Write a letter to a school nurse. Use your own paper. Report on the health of your child
or a child you know. Use at least four list words.

Proofread your letter carefully and correct any mistakes. Then make a clean copy and
put it in your writing portfolio.

Start Early

Ⓐ Check the Meaning

Read the paragraphs below. Think about the meaning of the words in bold type.

Caring for a child should begin after the child's **conception**. It makes sense, therefore, for a woman to check with a doctor if there is any **suspicion** that she is expecting a child. This may be weeks before her body begins to change its **appearance**. A doctor or clinic will help her **acquire** the information needed to protect her baby's health. Often a woman will receive a **brochure** explaining certain precautions she should take. For example, she will need to watch her **diet**. Gaining too much weight can cause problems during delivery. No pills or other medicines should be taken without a doctor's approval. In addition, the doctor may wish to review both parents' medical histories. The doctor might also do certain tests on the unborn child. Such tests look for problems resulting from the child's **heredity**.

Equally important is learning how to be a parent. Many clinics provide **instruction** in parenting skills. New parents can learn basic **hygiene** so that they and their child stay healthy. Developing a few healthy habits early on can result in **permanent** improvements for both parents and child. These classes also help parents spot certain danger signs. Newborn children cry when they are hungry and when they are in pain. It is important to know the difference. Then you will know when the child needs **relief** from any suffering. If you seek **immediate** attention for small problems, you can avoid larger ones.

Check the Meaning

Choose the correct meaning for the word in bold type. Fill in the circle next to the correct meaning.

1. **Hygiene** is
   - Ⓐ a type of animal.
   - Ⓑ someone who grants wishes.
   - Ⓒ practices that promote good health.
   - Ⓓ a very active adult.

2. A **brochure** is a
   - Ⓐ pamphlet.
   - Ⓑ green vegetable.
   - Ⓒ small piece of coal.
   - Ⓓ large pin worn by women.

3. If you have a **suspicion**, you
   - Ⓐ are easily influenced by others.
   - Ⓑ suspect or think something is true.
   - Ⓒ will soon become ill.
   - Ⓓ are over six feet tall.

4. The **conception** of a child is its
   - Ⓐ initial formation in the mother's womb.
   - Ⓑ demands made on a parent.
   - Ⓒ birth.
   - Ⓓ ability to think.

5. A person's **appearance** is
   - Ⓐ his or her attitude.
   - Ⓑ the way he or she looks.
   - Ⓒ the thing that makes him or her happy.
   - Ⓓ the way he or she sees others.

6. A **permanent** improvement
   - Ⓐ requires a large amount of money.
   - Ⓑ is difficult to notice.
   - Ⓒ is one that is unfinished.
   - Ⓓ is not expected to change.

7. When people **acquire** good habits, they
   - Ⓐ teach them to others.
   - Ⓑ do not need them.
   - Ⓒ get or obtain them.
   - Ⓓ tell others about them.

8. When people seek **relief**, they
   - Ⓐ try to reduce pain or distress.
   - Ⓑ look for bargains.
   - Ⓒ replace plants and trees after a storm.
   - Ⓓ study a new subject.

9. Your **heredity** is
   - Ⓐ the things passed on to you by your parents.
   - Ⓑ the money you get from your parents.
   - Ⓒ what others say about you.
   - Ⓓ your personal taste.

10. A **diet** is
    - Ⓐ a type of exercise.
    - Ⓑ the foods one eats.
    - Ⓒ a frightening adventure.
    - Ⓓ the fear of flying.

11. **Immediate** attention is
    - Ⓐ carelessly given.
    - Ⓑ given right away.
    - Ⓒ unfairly divided.
    - Ⓓ reported to the police.

12. **Instruction** is
    - Ⓐ a type of savings account.
    - Ⓑ a way of making heat.
    - Ⓒ rude behavior.
    - Ⓓ teaching something to another person.

Score: /12

Ⓑ Study the Spelling

Word List

immediate	instruction	acquire	diet
heredity	hygiene	conception	relief
suspicion	brochure	appearance	permanent

Write the list word or words for each clue.

1. It has two syllables and four letters. _____

2. They have an *ie* in the second syllable.

_____   _____

3. It ends with *ent*. _____

4. They end with *tion*. _____   _____

5. The vowel in the first syllable is *y*. _____

6. It is formed from the word *appear*. _____

7. Change the first two letters in *destruction* to make this word.

_____

8. It rhymes with *nutrition*, but it has no *t* in its spelling. _____

9. It begins with two consonants and rhymes with *impure*.

_____

10. It is formed from the word *conceive*. _____

11. Change two letters in *require* to make this word. _____

12. They come between *heredity* and *instruction* in the dictionary.

_____   _____

One word in each group is misspelled. Circle the misspelled word, and then write it correctly.

13. acquire   immediate   broshure   _____

14. relief   appearence   permanent   _____

15. instruction   diet   hygeine   _____

16. suspicion   heredity   concepition   _____

Score: ⁄ 16

C Build Your Skills

Language Tutor

A suffix is a word part added to the end of the word. Some suffixes are used to change the way a word is used. The *-ion* and *-ance* suffixes change a word from an action word, or verb, to a naming word, or noun. A final *e* in a word is dropped before adding *-ion* or *-ance*.

Action Word	Suffix	Naming Word
instruct	-ion	instruction
appear	-ance	appearance
locate	-ion	location

Find the missing word in the second sentence by adding a suffix to the underlined word in the first sentence. Write the second sentence.

1. Many people will <u>attend</u> the meeting. The _____ should be good.

_____

2. The city will <u>elect</u> a new town clerk. An _____ is scheduled for Tuesday.

_____

3. You must <u>act</u> quickly to get a ticket. Immediate _____ is necessary because the tickets will sell out soon.

_____

4. The nurse will <u>assist</u> you when you arrive. The _____ will be of great help to us.

_____

5. This station will <u>televise</u> the big game. You can see it on _____.

_____

6. Please help me <u>correct</u> the mistakes in my paper. The _____ will help my grade.

_____

Ⓓ Proofread and Write

Jackie wrote some questions to ask her doctor on her next visit. She made four spelling mistakes. Cross out the misspelled words. Write the correct spellings above them.

> Questions for Dr. Vance
>
> **1.** Should my diat include meat and fish?
>
> **2.** Where can I get instruction in how to feed a baby?
>
> **3.** Will the hereditey of my baby affect its appearance?
>
> **4.** How long is it from conception to birth?
>
> **5.** Will any weight I gain be permenent?
>
> **6.** Where can I acquire a brochure on hygeine?

Make a list of questions to ask your doctor on your next visit. Use at least four list words.

_____

_____

_____

_____

_____

_____

Writing Portfolio

Proofread your questions carefully and correct any mistakes. Then make a clean copy and put it in your writing portfolio.

Staying Healthy

Ⓐ Check the Meaning

Read the paragraph below. Think about the meaning of the words in bold type.

At home, under the care of a parent or **guardian**, children are safe from many ills. As children grow up, however, they begin to **encounter** life outside the home. In their first **kindergarten** classroom, children are **exposed** to everything from head lice to the flu. Some childhood diseases are not serious. The common cold or mild flu is usually no cause for alarm. A normal, healthy child will build up a **resistance** to such things and fight them off in time. Other, more serious, diseases need added protection. This often takes the form of shots that make children **immune** to serious diseases like polio and certain types of measles. Schools require proof of such immunity before a child may come to class. Check with your doctor and your school to be sure your children are immune from such diseases.

Choose the correct meaning for the word in bold type. Fill in the circle next to the correct meaning.

1. When people are **exposed** to something, they are
- Ⓐ holding on to it.
- Ⓑ controlling it.
- Ⓒ rejecting it.
- Ⓓ in its presence.

2. Resistance is
- Ⓐ a forceful demand.
- Ⓑ the ability to reject.
- Ⓒ a talent for writing.
- Ⓓ an extra supply of something.

3. When people are **immune** to a disease, they
- Ⓐ are likely to get it.
- Ⓑ are protected from it.
- Ⓒ are unaware of it.
- Ⓓ have had it several times.

4. A **guardian**
- Ⓐ cares for another person.
- Ⓑ works at a prison.
- Ⓒ is proof that something works.
- Ⓓ is a burial ground.

5. To **encounter** something is to
- Ⓐ hide behind it.
- Ⓑ overcome it.
- Ⓒ meet it.
- Ⓓ surrender to it.

6. Kindergarten is
- Ⓐ an area with many trees.
- Ⓑ a type of food.
- Ⓒ a class for very young children.
- Ⓓ a group of teachers.

Check the Meaning

Read the paragraph below. Think about the meaning of the words in bold type.

Health and fitness are not just for young people. They are for anyone willing to accept the **discipline** of a good diet and regular **exercise**. With age there is a **tendency** to feel that the body is no longer able to perform. Aches and pains are considered normal. Instead of pushing the body to do more, activities become limited. Yet example after example shows us that older people can—and should—be active. Men and women in their sixties have run in marathons, races of more than twenty-six miles. Some **professional** athletes stay **competitive** into their forties and fifties. For most people, simple activities like walking and swimming are all that is needed to stay in shape. It's important to include exercise in your daily **routine**. In the winter, do push-ups, sit-ups, and other indoor exercises. Of course, such exercises will be of little use if you follow them with soda and chips.

Choose the correct meaning for the word in bold type. Fill in the circle next to the correct meaning.

7. If you have a **tendency** to do something, you
- Ⓐ have lost the desire for doing it.
- Ⓑ are likely to do it.
- Ⓒ are very good at doing it.
- Ⓓ have lost the ability to do it.

8. Your **routine** is made up of
- Ⓐ the rooms in your home.
- Ⓑ all the property you own.
- Ⓒ people who follow your example.
- Ⓓ the things you do over and over.

9. People who are **competitive**,
- Ⓐ do not make friends easily.
- Ⓑ are able to keep up with others in a contest.
- Ⓒ say kind and generous things about others.
- Ⓓ are easily confused.

10. Discipline is
- Ⓐ a person who follows another's teachings.
- Ⓑ an argument.
- Ⓒ the ability to control your actions.
- Ⓓ the loss of all hope.

11. A **professional** athlete
- Ⓐ plays a sport for money.
- Ⓑ has few skills.
- Ⓒ is anyone who loves a sport.
- Ⓓ cheers loudly at a game.

12. Exercise is
- Ⓐ the release of air from the lungs.
- Ⓑ an activity that strengthens the body.
- Ⓒ a means of driving away evil spirits.
- Ⓓ a good example of something.

Score: 12

Ⓑ Study the Spelling

> **Word List**
>
> | resistance | professional | exposed | immune |
> | discipline | routine | competitive | guardian |
> | encounter | tendency | exercise | kindergarten |

Write the list word that is formed from each of these words.

1. resist _____

2. expose _____

3. compete _____

4. profession _____

5. guard _____

Write the list word or words for each clue.

6. They end with *ine*. _____ _____

7. They have a double consonant in their spelling.

_____ _____

8. They begin with the *ex-* prefix. _____ _____

9. It begins like *tender* and ends like *fancy*. _____

10. It comes from the German word *Kinder*, meaning "children," and *Garten*, meaning "garden." _____

11. The word *count* is part of its spelling. _____

12. The second letter in its spelling is a silent *u*. _____

13. They have two syllables.

_____ _____ _____

Add the missing syllable. Write the list word.

14. rou_____ _____

15. disci_____ _____

16. guardi_____ _____

Ⓒ Build Your Skills

Language Tutor

A suffix is a word part added to the end of a word. It adds meaning to the word or changes how the word is used. One type of suffix adds the meaning "one who" or "that which" to a word.

Suffix	Meaning	Example
-ian, -or, and -ist	one who	guardian, one who guards
	one who specializes in (something)	dentist, one who specializes in dental work
-er	that which	copier, that which copies
	one who	volunteer, one who offers or volunteers

The underlined word in each sentence contains a suffix meaning "one who" or "that which." Study the word and the sentence. Then write a short definition for the underlined word.

1. The <u>conductor</u> walked onto the stage ready to begin the concert.

_____

2. After weeks of practice, the <u>musician</u> was ready to perform.

_____

3. If you cannot find a book, ask the <u>librarian</u> for help.

_____

4. The garage used a <u>computer</u> to time the engine.

_____

5. An <u>electrician</u> must do the work on the lights.

_____

6. That painting was done by Cahoon, a famous <u>artist</u>.

_____

7. The <u>actor</u> received an award for his work in the movie.

_____

8. We use a <u>humidifier</u> in the winter because the air is very dry.

_____

Score: 8

D Proofread and Write

The following rules for good health appeared on posters at a clinic. There are four spelling mistakes on the posters. Cross out the misspelled words. Write the correct spellings above them.

Make exercise part of your daily routeen.

If you have been exposd to the Asian flu, see a doctor at the clinic.

Are your children immune to polio?

If not, see a health care professional before they start kindergarden.

A good diet builds resistence to disease.

Writing Portfolio

Make some posters about good health. Use your own paper. Use at least four list words.

Proofread your posters carefully and correct any mistakes. Then make clean copies and put them in your writing portfolio.

Unit 2 Review

Finish the Meaning

Fill in the circle next to the word that best completes each sentence.

1. Hair and eye color are the result of _____.

   Ⓐ diet   Ⓒ negligence
   Ⓑ heredity   Ⓓ appetite

2. Always ask for an _____ bill when you have your car repaired.

   Ⓐ injury   Ⓒ itemized
   Ⓑ exercise   Ⓓ exposed

3. Many schools ask a parent or _____ for a note if a child has missed school.

   Ⓐ guardian   Ⓒ professional
   Ⓑ patience   Ⓓ guarantee

4. It is a good idea to go to a doctor once a year for a(n) _____ exam.

   Ⓐ physical   Ⓒ artificial
   Ⓑ fatigue   Ⓓ permanent

5. No one should share _____ information about another person.

   Ⓐ competitive   Ⓒ obvious
   Ⓑ precise   Ⓓ confidential

6. It takes time for children to develop a _____ to germs.

   Ⓐ stamina   Ⓒ resistance
   Ⓑ patience   Ⓓ precaution

7. Develop this habit of good _____: wash your hands before eating.

   Ⓐ honor   Ⓒ hygiene
   Ⓑ instruction   Ⓓ insurance

8. A check is not good without a _____ on it.

   Ⓐ balance   Ⓒ receipt
   Ⓑ signature   Ⓓ technique

9. It will take Sam about six weeks to _____ after his operation.

   Ⓐ accommodate   Ⓒ exploit
   Ⓑ exercise   Ⓓ recuperate

10. The _____ tells you all you need to know about your VCR.

    Ⓐ brochure   Ⓒ inquiry
    Ⓑ balance   Ⓓ insurance

11. Ask for help if you _____ any problems.

    Ⓐ avoid   Ⓒ redeem
    Ⓑ restrict   Ⓓ encounter

12. It is easy to get into debt, so _____ your credit card bill carefully.

    Ⓐ monitor   Ⓒ accept
    Ⓑ exercise   Ⓓ embarrass

GO ON ▶

Check the Spelling

Fill in the circle next to the word that is spelled correctly and best completes each sentence.

13. My _____ is an expert on heart problems.

- Ⓐ phisician
- Ⓒ physician
- Ⓑ physisian
- Ⓓ physicion

14. A bad cut or broken bone needs _____ attention.

- Ⓐ immediate
- Ⓒ immedeate
- Ⓑ imeddiate
- Ⓓ immeddiate

15. The first day of _____ is a big day for children and parents.

- Ⓐ kindergarden
- Ⓒ kindagarten
- Ⓑ kindergardin
- Ⓓ kindergarten

16. The blood was sent to a _____ for testing.

- Ⓐ labratory
- Ⓒ laboratorie
- Ⓑ laboratoury
- Ⓓ laboratory

17. It takes _____ to give up smoking.

- Ⓐ disciplin
- Ⓒ discipline
- Ⓑ disipline
- Ⓓ discaplin

18. If you have more work than you can do, hire an _____.

- Ⓐ asisstant
- Ⓒ assistent
- Ⓑ assistant
- Ⓓ assisstant

19. Make a budget if you have a _____ to overspend.

- Ⓐ tendency
- Ⓒ tendendie
- Ⓑ tendancy
- Ⓓ tendensy

20. Do not buy meat that smells bad or that has a bad _____.

- Ⓐ apearrance
- Ⓒ appearence
- Ⓑ apperance
- Ⓓ appearance

21. Heart _____ is a leading cause of death in this country.

- Ⓐ disese
- Ⓒ disease
- Ⓑ dasease
- Ⓓ diseese

22. The _____ department helps all new employees.

- Ⓐ personnel
- Ⓒ persenel
- Ⓑ personelle
- Ⓓ pursennel

23. Tina never had a _____ we were planning a surprise party.

- Ⓐ suspition
- Ⓒ suspetion
- Ⓑ suspishen
- Ⓓ suspicion

24. Some doctors charge a _____ fee if you miss an appointment.

- Ⓐ cancellation
- Ⓒ canncelation
- Ⓑ cansellation
- Ⓓ cancelation

Score: ___/24

Beat the Crowd

Ⓐ Check the Meaning

Read the paragraphs below. Think about the meaning of the words in bold type.

For most people, searching for a job can be discouraging. Seeing long lines of people waiting to apply for one or two jobs can lead to **frustration**. When hundreds of people **pursue** the same job, your chances seem small. Keeping up your search in such a situation requires great **commitment**.

There are ways to improve your chances, however. An **adept** job hunter can find **available** jobs that others may overlook. Everyone knows to check the newspaper ads. Yet many jobs are not advertised. Talk to your friends. Often they will know of an opening where they work. By applying for it before it is advertised in the newspaper, you improve your chances. An employer will **perceive** your ability to get there first as a **positive** sign. Another source of job information might be technical or **vocational** schools, where **manual** skills like carpentry and other trades are taught. Employers frequently seek workers there. A bulletin board may list many openings that aren't advertised in the newspaper. Another good place to look is a community college. Community colleges often provide employment services. By enrolling in a class, you may be able to use this service to search for a job.

Sometimes the key is being able to **adapt** your skills to an employer's needs. A good waiter or waitress will probably be quite **competent** in any customer service position. Grocery stores, banks, and government offices need people who treat customers well. Your résumé or application should therefore **address** the skills you have, not the jobs you have held.

Check the Meaning

Choose the correct meaning for the word in bold type. Fill in the circle next to the correct answer.

1. If you **adapt** your skills, you
   - (A) teach them to another person.
   - (B) forget them.
   - (C) hide them.
   - (D) change them to fit a new situation.

2. If something is **available**, it
   - (A) has been broken.
   - (B) can be provided.
   - (C) costs a large amount of money.
   - (D) is light and easy to carry.

3. A **commitment** is
   - (A) a strong feeling to do something.
   - (B) a place to hold criminals.
   - (C) a job done by a group of people.
   - (D) payment for work.

4. **Manual** skills
   - (A) must be done by men.
   - (B) are those that are easily learned.
   - (C) make computers unnecessary.
   - (D) require the use of the hands.

5. A **vocational** school
   - (A) has a long vacation period.
   - (B) admits only very young children.
   - (C) trains people in the skilled trades.
   - (D) is one with large classes.

6. A **positive** sign is one that
   - (A) surprises someone.
   - (B) is favorable.
   - (C) is difficult to understand.
   - (D) expresses a funny idea.

7. **Frustration** is
   - (A) a feeling that you can never win.
   - (B) pride about what you can do.
   - (C) the ability to trick or fool others.
   - (D) love for one's job.

8. If you **address** something, you
   - (A) ignore it.
   - (B) plant it in the ground.
   - (C) deal with it directly.
   - (D) admire it.

9. A **competent** person
   - (A) requires medical treatment.
   - (B) is overweight.
   - (C) lacks the ability to read and write.
   - (D) can do a task very well.

10. If you **pursue** something, you
    - (A) chase after it.
    - (B) have it arrested.
    - (C) damage it.
    - (D) recommend it to a friend.

11. If a person is **adept**, he or she is
    - (A) easily confused.
    - (B) often ill.
    - (C) skillful.
    - (D) uncertain about things.

12. If you **perceive** something, you
    - (A) change it.
    - (B) become aware of it.
    - (C) sell it at a high price.
    - (D) use it in a selfish way.

Score: /12

B Study the Spelling

Word List

adapt	positive	commitment	available	address	competent
frustration	adept	manual	pursue	vocational	perceive

Write the list word or words for each clue.

1. They end with *al*. _____ _____

2. It begins with two consonants and ends with *ion*. _____

3. It has two sets of double consonants. _____

4. They end with *ent*. _____ _____

5. It rhymes with *receive*. _____

6. They have two syllables and five letters. Four of the letters are the same.

_____ _____

7. It begins like *position* and ends like *adjective*. _____

8. It rhymes with *canoe*. _____

Write the four list words that begin with *a*. Write them in alphabetical order.

9. _____   11. _____

10. _____   12. _____

Add the missing vowels. Write the list word.

13. m___n___ ___l _____

14. p___rs___ ___ _____

15. c___mp___t___nt _____

16. p___rc___ ___v___ _____

One word in each group is misspelled. Circle the misspelled word, then write it correctly.

17. available   competent   committment   _____

18. manuel   pursue   vocational   _____

19. frustration   percieve   adapt   _____

20. adept   addres   positive   _____

Score: 20

Ⓒ Build Your Skills

Language Tutor

A sentence is a group of words that expresses a thought completely. It begins with a capital letter and ends with a period, a question mark, or an exclamation point.

A statement ends with a period. Jack is a competent plumber.

A question ends with a question mark. Did he fix your sink?

An exclamation ends with an exclamation point. Come quickly!

Turn each group of words into the type of sentence stated. Add capital letters and end punctuation. The first one is done for you.

1. Statement: a long line of people

A long line of people waited for the office to open.

2. Question: an ad in the newspaper

_____

3. Statement: a good vocational school

_____

4. Exclamation: a pay raise

_____

5. Question: bulletin board

_____

6. Statement: job skills

_____

7. Statement: manual skills

_____

8. Question: feeling of frustration

_____

D Proofread and Write

The following notice was placed on the bulletin board at a factory. It has four spelling mistakes. Cross out the misspelled words. Write the correct spellings above them.

WANTED:

THREE COMPATENT WORKERS

Duties: Do simple repairs and other types of manual labor in

large factory.

Skills Needed: Should be adapt with tools and machines.

Training at a vacational school a plus.

Must be available to work weekends.

A pasitive attitude and a commitment to

learning our business is very important.

Rewards: Good pay and benefits.

Write an ad for a job you would like to have. Include the duties, the skills needed, and the rewards. Use at least four list words. Then write an answer to the ad on another piece of paper.

_____

_____

_____

_____

_____

_____

Writing Portfolio

Proofread your job ad and your answer carefully. Correct any mistakes. Then make clean copies of them and put them in your writing portfolio.

The Modern Office

Ⓐ Check the Meaning

Read the paragraphs below. Think about the meaning of the words in bold type.

Once it was possible to get an office job just by knowing how to type. The typewriter and the telephone were the most **complicated** machines in the office. Now, however, things are very different. The typewriter has all but disappeared. In its place is a new **device**, the computer. Even the telephone has changed. It no longer is just for talking to people outside the office. Now it is used to **transmit** letters and other documents across town or around the world.

A smart worker will not **view** computers as a problem when looking for office work. There is nothing very **mysterious** about them. Think of a computer as you would a car. Only a few people know how they work, but nearly everyone can drive. So unless you plan to do your own **maintenance**, you can probably learn about computers very quickly.

Choose the correct meaning for the word in bold type. Fill in the circle next to the correct answer.

1. To **view** is to
Ⓐ look at.
Ⓑ reward.
Ⓒ improve.
Ⓓ repair.

2. Maintenance is
Ⓐ the most important part of anything.
Ⓑ the work of keeping things running.
Ⓒ a part of a computer.
Ⓓ a type of office machine.

3. If you **transmit** a letter, you
Ⓐ type it.
Ⓑ send it someplace.
Ⓒ translate it into another language.
Ⓓ copy it.

4. A **device** is a
Ⓐ funny story.
Ⓑ suggestion.
Ⓒ machine or gadget.
Ⓓ bomb.

5. If something is **mysterious**, it is
Ⓐ sleepy.
Ⓑ plain and simple.
Ⓒ a failure.
Ⓓ difficult to understand.

6. A **complicated** machine
Ⓐ never needs repairs.
Ⓑ has many confusing parts.
Ⓒ is spoken of very kindly.
Ⓓ requires several people to operate.

Check the Meaning

When sales are slow and costs rising, employers may decide to **downsize** their workforce. Unfortunately, this is not an **infrequent** event. Large companies may lay off hundreds of workers at a time. The best **strategy** for avoiding a layoff is to have the skills that employers need. This may mean learning the latest **software**, the programs that make the computers do work for you. Take advantage of any training programs offered by your employer. Today's workers must also learn to be **flexible**. Learn how to do several different jobs. If your job is no longer needed, your employer might be able to offer you an **alternate** position. However, you must first show that you really can do another job. The time when one job lasts a lifetime may be over. Today the well-prepared worker knows how to deal with change.

Choose the correct meaning for the word in bold type. Fill in the circle next to the correct answer.

7. If you **downsize** something, you make it
(A) larger.
(B) prettier.
(C) smaller.
(D) simpler.

8. If something is **flexible**, it
(A) has a sweet flavor.
(B) bends or changes easily.
(C) burns easily.
(D) floats.

9. A **strategy** is
(A) a layer of dirt.
(B) an illegal action.
(C) payment made to an organization.
(D) a plan of action.

10. An **infrequent** event
(A) marks a holiday.
(B) usually makes a lot of noise.
(C) is very informative.
(D) does not happen very often.

11. Software
(A) is a type of clothing.
(B) controls what a computer does.
(C) is used in making furniture.
(D) uses the sun's energy.

12. An **alternate** position is
(A) one offered in place of another.
(B) any high-paying job.
(C) one requiring no skill.
(D) one that lasts only a short time.

B Study the Spelling

Word List

downsize	maintenance	infrequent	view	device	flexible
software	mysterious	transmit	complicated	strategy	alternate

Form a list word by matching the beginning of a word in the first column with its ending in the second column. Write the list word.

mainten	ous	1. _____
flex	ance	2. _____
alter	size	3. _____
mysteri	ible	4. _____
soft	ware	5. _____
down	nate	6. _____

Write the list word or words for each clue.

7. It has four letters and one syllable. _____

8. The word *ice* is part of its spelling. _____

9. It begins with three consonants. _____

10. It begins with a prefix that means "not." _____

11. It ends with *ed*. _____

12. It is formed from the word *mystery*. _____

13. It is formed from the word *maintain*. _____

14. Change two letters in *advice* to make this word. _____

Write *transmit, infrequent, downsize,* and *alternate* in alphabetical order. Use dots between the syllables.

15. _____   17. _____

16. _____   18. _____

C Build Your Skills

Language Tutor

Always capitalize a person's name and title.

We met the doctor.	Make an appointment with <u>D</u>octor <u>J</u>udith <u>J</u>ensen.
There is a message for the captain.	An award was given to <u>C</u>aptain <u>P</u>arker.
The man waited on us.	The manager is <u>M</u>r. <u>D</u>. <u>J</u>. <u>W</u>alker.
This woman will try the case.	Please report to <u>J</u>udge <u>L</u>isa <u>G</u>oldman.

Write each sentence. Capitalize the names and titles.

1. A new strategy was developed by coach johnson.

_____

2. Ask mr. rogers to transmit a message to helen fisher.

_____

3. The president of the company promised doctor potter that she would not downsize the department.

_____

4. Your aunt tanya knows how to use the new software.

_____

5. The governor met with senator winston smith.

_____

6. I expect to be in professor rivera's class tomorrow.

_____

7. Tell ms. tina wing to come in.

_____

8. Our new minister is reverend steven burger.

_____

Score: /8

D Proofread and Write

Josh met with an employment counselor. He wrote these notes on the things he was told. He made three spelling mistakes. He also forgot to capitalize one word. Cross out the misspelled words and the word that should have been capitalized. Write the words correctly above them.

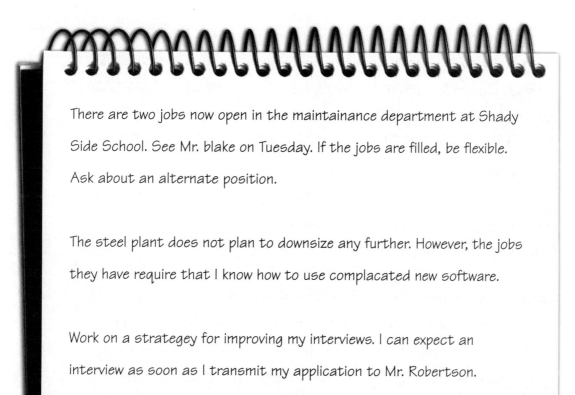

There are two jobs now open in the maintainance department at Shady Side School. See Mr. blake on Tuesday. If the jobs are filled, be flexible. Ask about an alternate position.

The steel plant does not plan to downsize any further. However, the jobs they have require that I know how to use complacated new software.

Work on a strategey for improving my interviews. I can expect an interview as soon as I transmit my application to Mr. Robertson.

Read the paragraphs on pages 61 and 62 again. Write some notes on the advice given there. Use at least four list words.

_____

_____

_____

_____

_____

_____

Writing Portfolio

Proofread your notes carefully and correct any mistakes. Then make a clean copy and put it in your writing portfolio.

11 Know Your Benefits

A Check the Meaning

Read the paragraphs below. Think about the meaning of the words in bold type.

One of the first things workers ask about a job is how much it pays. Nowadays, however, the benefits an employer provides are as important as the **wages** he or she pays. A wise employee will carefully study all available benefits to take advantage of them. Start by visiting the personnel department and talking with the people who **administer** the plans. You may have the **option** of selecting from among several health insurance plans. The cost and coverage may differ with each plan. The best plan for you will depend on your **personal** situation. Consider the size of your family, the health of each member, and your ability to pay the cost.

Some employers also offer insurance that will pay all or part of your wages if you suffer a **severe disability** and are unable to work. The cost of this coverage may be small. If you provide the only income for your family, this insurance can be very important to have. It is worth every penny to know that you are covered if you suffer a severe injury one day.

The **typical** employer allows employees a **realistic** number of days off for illness. Some will also allow an employee to take time off for other **compelling** reasons, such as a death in the family. To be paid for these days off, an employee may need to follow a certain **procedure**. Know what your employer allows and how you can take advantage of this benefit.

You may have the choice of joining a union. If so, your employer may **deduct** the dues from your paycheck. If you choose not to join, you may still be required to pay a fee to the union. This fee pays the union to **negotiate** a contract for you and other workers.

Check the Meaning

Choose the correct meaning for the word in bold type. Fill in the circle next to the correct answer.

1. If you **administer** a plan, you
   - (A) ruin it.
   - (B) change it.
   - (C) discard it.
   - (D) direct it.

2. A **procedure** is a
   - (A) way of doing something.
   - (B) group of people walking together.
   - (C) type of prize or reward.
   - (D) term used in grammar.

3. A **typical** employer is one that
   - (A) has just started a business.
   - (B) is like many other employers.
   - (C) provides no benefits.
   - (D) is going out of business.

4. **Wages** are
   - (A) the cost of health insurance.
   - (B) the money paid for work or services.
   - (C) bets made on sporting events.
   - (D) time lost due to illness.

5. Another word for **option** is
   - (A) opinion.
   - (B) expense.
   - (C) choice.
   - (D) dishonor.

6. If you **negotiate**, you
   - (A) delay an action.
   - (B) use mathematics to solve a problem.
   - (C) plan a meeting.
   - (D) discuss an agreement with someone.

7. If someone has a **disability**, he or she
   - (A) cannot do certain physical activities.
   - (B) has little money.
   - (C) loves the outdoors.
   - (D) does a job well.

8. A **compelling** reason is one that is
   - (A) weak and questionable.
   - (B) quickly dismissed.
   - (C) humorous.
   - (D) strong and forceful.

9. Another word for **severe** is
   - (A) simple.
   - (B) hidden.
   - (C) serious.
   - (D) healthy.

10. If something is **realistic**, it is
    - (A) reasonable and sensible.
    - (B) ready for use.
    - (C) disorderly.
    - (D) colorful.

11. A **personal** matter is one that
    - (A) is well known.
    - (B) cannot be easily explained.
    - (C) concerns you as a person.
    - (D) must be settled in court.

12. If you **deduct** something, you
    - (A) lose it.
    - (B) add it.
    - (C) subtract it.
    - (D) double it.

Score: ___ / 12

B Study the Spelling

Word List

negotiate	administer	option	procedure	compelling	severe
wages	typical	deduct	disability	personal	realistic

Write the list word for each clue.

1. It begins with the *dis-* prefix. _____

2. It contains a double consonant. _____

3. It is formed from the word *proceed*. _____

4. The word *real* is part of its spelling. _____

5. It is the plural form of a word. _____

6. The word *person* is part of its spelling. _____

7. The vowel in its first syllable is *y*. _____

8. The word *minister* is part of its spelling. _____

9. It has the *-ion* suffix. _____

10. It begins like *seven* and ends like *here*. _____

Circle the list word you find in each of these words. Then write the word.

11. optional _____

12. deduction _____

13. renegotiate _____

14. typically _____

15. unrealistic _____

16. personality _____

One word in each group is misspelled. Circle the misspelled word, then write it correctly.

17. administer   nagotiate   option   _____

18. option   proceedure   compelling   _____

19. personnal   realistic   disability   _____

20. wages   typecal   deduct   _____

Score: 20

ⒸBuild Your Skills

Language Tutor

Nouns name persons, places, things, or ideas. A proper noun names a particular person, place, thing, or idea. A proper noun always begins with a capital letter.

Common Noun	Proper Noun
a country	France
religion	Protestantism, Protestant congregation
club	the Girl Scouts of America
holiday	Labor Day

Copy these sentences. Begin each proper noun with a capital letter.

1. We visited several countries, but I like the united kingdom the best.

_____

2. The south side bowling club will meet in the baptist church.

_____

3. I must work on the fourth of july this year.

_____

4. What is the procedure for enrolling at western driving school?

_____

Copy these sentences. Replace the underlined word with a proper noun.

5. That religious group is building a new church.

_____

6. My wife grew up in a city.

_____

7. Jack plans to run for president of that club.

_____

8. After high school, my son wants to attend a college.

_____

D Proofread and Write

Rita wrote these questions so that she would remember to ask her new employer. She made four spelling mistakes. Cross out the misspelled words. Write the correct spellings above them.

How often are your employees paid their wages?

Do I have the option of coming to work early so that I can leave early?

What is the pracedure for locking up at night?

Does the union negotiaet for all workers?

Is it reelistic to expect a raise after six months?

Does the typical worker choose to buy disabilty insurance?

Write some questions you might want to ask a possible employer. Use at least four list words.

_____

_____

_____

_____

_____

_____

Writing Portfolio

Proofread your questions carefully and correct any mistakes. Then make a clean copy and put it in your writing portfolio.

Managing the Work

Ⓐ Check the Meaning

Read the paragraph below. Think about the meaning of the words in bold type.

If you want something done right, do it yourself. You have no doubt heard that often. If you are a manager, you are **responsible** for the work many people do. You just cannot do it all yourself. Instead, you must see that those who work for you do the job right. First you need to know the **quantity** of work to be done. Then you must **gauge** the time, tools, and people needed to do it. The key is often being able to get the most from each worker. **Encourage** workers by praising them when they do a good job or when they suggest a **solution** to a problem. By including everyone in important decisions, you will raise the **morale** in the workplace. Workers who feel that they are valued work harder and smarter.

Choose the correct meaning for the word in bold type. Fill in the circle next to the correct answer.

1. When people **gauge** something, they
   Ⓐ promise that it will work.
   Ⓑ figure its measurements.
   Ⓒ grab it firmly.
   Ⓓ watch it secretly.

2. A **solution** is
   Ⓐ a period of time.
   Ⓑ a person who sleeps soundly.
   Ⓒ an answer to a problem.
   Ⓓ a steep hillside.

3. To **encourage** workers is to
   Ⓐ give them hope and support.
   Ⓑ criticize their work.
   Ⓒ send them away.
   Ⓓ refuse to pay them.

4. To be **responsible** for something is to
   Ⓐ know little about it.
   Ⓑ fix it.
   Ⓒ break it into smaller parts.
   Ⓓ be praised or blamed for how it turns out.

5. If you raise **morale,** you
   Ⓐ improve the mood and frame of mind.
   Ⓑ provide religious instruction.
   Ⓒ create a sense of gloom.
   Ⓓ do away with all rules.

6. Another word for **quantity** is
   Ⓐ kind.
   Ⓑ amount.
   Ⓒ difficulty.
   Ⓓ attention.

Check the Meaning

Read the paragraph below. Think about the meaning of the words in bold type.

Have you ever seen a **diagram** of a company or business? At the top of this chart is the president or general manager. He or she has the final **authority** for all big decisions. Below the president are two or more managers. Each is responsible for a part of the **business**. One might watch over the development of new ideas. Another might follow the costs and the sales. Another might be in charge of the plant where the products are made. Everyone's role in the company is included in such a chart. A chart of this type is useful because it shows how a person's work is connected to the work of a **colleague** in another department. In large companies it can be difficult to see the importance of your work. The chart shows how you **cooperate** with other workers in other departments to make a successful business. Workers who **persist** in thinking only about what they do, and not what the company does, will soon be dropped from the chart.

Choose the correct meaning for the word in bold type. Fill in the circle next to the correct answer.

7. A **business** is
- Ⓐ a large picture.
- Ⓑ a system of ropes and wheels.
- Ⓒ someone who bothers others.
- Ⓓ people organized to buy, sell, or make something.

8. If you **cooperate** with people, you
- Ⓐ do their work.
- Ⓑ work with them for a shared goal.
- Ⓒ compete against them.
- Ⓓ refuse their help.

9. A **diagram** is
- Ⓐ a drawing that shows how something works.
- Ⓑ a conversation between two people.
- Ⓒ an organ that helps one breathe.
- Ⓓ a type of prayer.

10. If you **persist** in doing something, you
- Ⓐ do it carefully.
- Ⓑ continue to do it.
- Ⓒ require help in doing it.
- Ⓓ do it for free.

11. A person with **authority**
- Ⓐ can answer all questions.
- Ⓑ has written many books.
- Ⓒ has the power to do something.
- Ⓓ is good with numbers.

12. A **colleague** is
- Ⓐ anyone who has gone to college.
- Ⓑ a co-worker.
- Ⓒ a large dog with a long nose.
- Ⓓ a supervisor or manager.

Score: / 12

B Study the Spelling

Word List

gauge	business	solution	colleague	quantity	morale
authority	encourage	diagram	cooperate	responsible	persist

Write the list word or words for each clue.

1. It has one syllable and five letters. _____

2. It ends with a double consonant. _____

3. The word *courage* is part of its spelling. _____

4. Add one letter to *moral* to make this word. _____

5. It is formed from the word *solve*. _____

6. It begins like *perfect* and ends like *insist*. _____

7. It has a double consonant and a silent *ue* in its spelling. _____

8. They end with *ity*. _____   _____

9. It has a double vowel that is pronounced as two different sounds.

   _____

10. It begins like *responsive* and ends like *flexible*. _____

Add the missing vowels. Write the list word.

11. c____ ____p____r____t____ _____

12. d____ ____gr____m _____

13. g____ ____g____ _____

14. ____ ____th____r____t____ _____

15. m____r____l____ _____

Write the list word from which these words were made.

16. quantities _____

17. persistent _____

18. encouragement _____

C Build Your Skills

Language Tutor

A business letter has six main parts: a heading with the return address and date, an inside address, a greeting, a body, a closing, and a signature. Study the example on the next page. Note that a comma is used to separate the date from the year and the city from the state.

The envelope also has a special form. The envelope below goes with the letter on the next page.

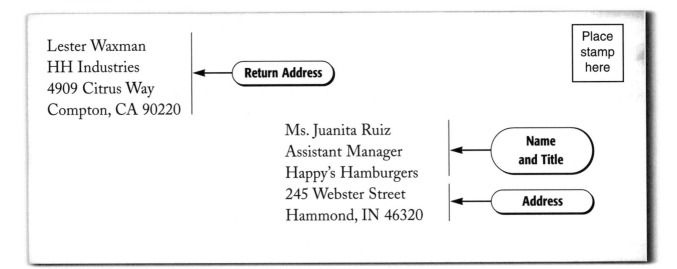

Study the envelope and the letter on the next page. Then answer these questions.

1. To whom is this letter being sent? _____

2. Who sent this letter? _____

3. For whom does Mr. Waxman work? _____

4. What is Mr. Waxman's position? _____

5. What is the abbreviation for California? _____

6. What kind of punctuation comes between the city and the state?

   _____

7. What kind of punctuation follows the greeting in the letter?

   _____

8. What kind of punctuation follows the closing in the letter?

   _____

Score: 8

ⓓ Proofread and Write

Mr. Waxman wrote this letter to one of his managers. He made four spelling mistakes. Cross out the misspelled words. Write the correct spellings above them.

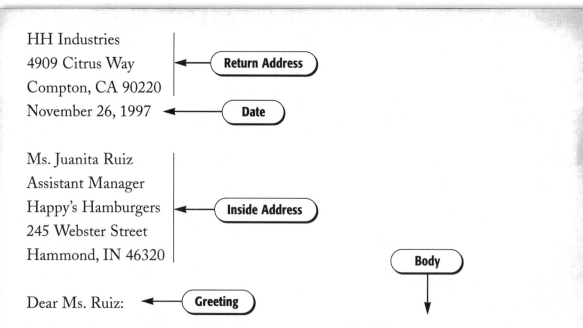

HH Industries
4909 Citrus Way ← **Return Address**
Compton, CA 90220
November 26, 1997 ← **Date**

Ms. Juanita Ruiz
Assistant Manager
Happy's Hamburgers ← **Inside Address**
245 Webster Street
Hammond, IN 46320

Body

Dear Ms. Ruiz: ← **Greeting**

I was very impressed by what I saw on my recent visit. Things are going much better since you began assisting the manager. You seem to have a found a salution to many problems. The moral of the workers is high. Best of all, the quantity of busness you are doing is way up.

I feel you are the person responsible for these improvements. I want to encerage you to persist in making these positive changes. You can be sure I will gladly cooperate with you in any way possible.

Sincerely, ← **Closing**

Lester Waxman ← **Signature**

Lester Waxman, Area Supervisor ← **Writer's Identification**

Writing Portfolio

Write a letter to a business or company. Use your own paper. You can thank the company for good service or point out a way to improve the business. Use at least four list words.

Proofread your letter carefully and correct any mistakes. Then make a clean copy to mail to the business or to put in your writing portfolio.

Unit 3 Review

Finish the Meaning

Fill in the circle next to the word that best completes each sentence.

1. Lou refused to give up. He would _____ until he achieved his goal.

   Ⓐ view   Ⓒ alternate
   Ⓑ persist Ⓓ investigate

2. Sometimes a simple machine is much better than a _____ one.

   Ⓐ complicated Ⓒ typical
   Ⓑ manual   Ⓓ responsible

3. A _____ worker does a job very well.

   Ⓐ maintenance Ⓒ clever
   Ⓑ confidential Ⓓ competent

4. We had twenty-five inches of rain this year. In a _____ year we get just sixteen inches.

   Ⓐ typical   Ⓒ duplicate
   Ⓑ realistic Ⓓ flexible

5. The personnel office will _____ the new program for employees.

   Ⓐ accumulate Ⓒ administer
   Ⓑ alternate   Ⓓ cooperate

6. After graduation, Sonya plans to _____ a career in teaching.

   Ⓐ redeem Ⓒ pursue
   Ⓑ deduct Ⓓ adapt

7. Next year this office will start a new _____. You will need to follow it.

   Ⓐ disability Ⓒ brochure
   Ⓑ procedure   Ⓓ precaution

8. Only people with the _____ to sign time cards should do so.

   Ⓐ authority Ⓒ technique
   Ⓑ patience   Ⓓ software

9. Kim improved her computer skills by taking classes at the _____ school.

   Ⓐ confidence   Ⓒ nutrition
   Ⓑ kindergarten Ⓓ vocational

10. If you want your children to succeed, _____ them to do their best.

    Ⓐ embarrass Ⓒ deduct
    Ⓑ encourage Ⓓ accommodate

11. Using the new machinery will reduce the need for _____ labor.

    Ⓐ appealing Ⓒ complicated
    Ⓑ manual   Ⓓ infrequent

12. Tina did not mind learning new tasks. She has always been quite _____.

    Ⓐ flexible Ⓒ remote
    Ⓑ severe   Ⓓ vague

GO ON ▶

Check the Spelling

Fill in the circle next to the word that is spelled correctly and best completes each sentence.

13. The dishwasher is a _____ for saving time and labor.

   Ⓐ davice   Ⓒ device
   Ⓑ davise   Ⓓ devise

14. You can often _____ the height of something by measuring its shadow.

   Ⓐ gaige   Ⓒ gayge
   Ⓑ gauge   Ⓓ guage

15. The nurses' union will _____ a contract with the hospital for next year.

   Ⓐ negotiate   Ⓒ nagoatiate
   Ⓑ nagotiate   Ⓓ neggotiate

16. By signing the pledge, you make a _____ to donate money.

   Ⓐ comittment   Ⓒ committment
   Ⓑ commitmint   Ⓓ commitment

17. Take care of _____ errands on your own time, not during the work day.

   Ⓐ personel   Ⓒ personal
   Ⓑ pursonal   Ⓓ personnal

18. Computers are not _____. One simply has to learn how to use them.

   Ⓐ mysterious   Ⓒ mystierous
   Ⓑ misterious   Ⓓ mistierious

19. The staff asked the government to _____ their concerns about worker safety.

   Ⓐ address   Ⓒ adres
   Ⓑ adress   Ⓓ addres

20. Although Chris sometimes disagrees with his _____, they make a great pair.

   Ⓐ colliegue   Ⓒ coleague
   Ⓑ colleage   Ⓓ colleague

21. The way you dress affects how others _____ you.

   Ⓐ purceive   Ⓒ percieve
   Ⓑ perceive   Ⓓ persieve

22. The coach was sure his new _____ would win the game.

   Ⓐ stradegy   Ⓒ stratejy
   Ⓑ strategy   Ⓓ strategie

23. Steve and his father have been in _____ together for more than twenty years.

   Ⓐ bussines   Ⓒ busines
   Ⓑ bizness   Ⓓ business

24. Jill had a _____ reason to miss work, so her boss gave her the day off.

   Ⓐ comppeling   Ⓒ commpeling
   Ⓑ compeling   Ⓓ compelling

13 The Library

Ⓐ Check the Meaning

Read the paragraphs below. Think about the meaning of the words in bold type.

You may have heard the familiar **proverb**, "A picture is worth a thousand words." Why choose one or the other? A modern library can offer both. While we usually think of the library as a place with books, it is really a source of much more. Some of the larger libraries lend framed copies of famous paintings. Paintings found in art **museums** can now be part of your home. Nearly all libraries now also offer movies on videotape. Many libraries also provide story hours for children after school and during the summer. Here both professional and **amateur** storytellers can **fascinate** their young listeners with everything from **ancient** folktales to modern horror stories.

Nevertheless, the library's main purpose is to offer the community many types of reading materials. In the library you will find copies of great **literature**, popular paperback books, and **magazines** on every possible topic. Are you interested in railroads? Cooking? Rock music? The library probably has a magazine for you.

Books, however, still take up most of the shelves in a library. Books are usually divided into two large groups. One group is referred to as **fiction**. These books contain made-up stories. They might be short stories or longer stories called **novels**. The other large group is nonfiction. An **autobiography**, a book in which a person tells the story of his or her life, falls into this group. Books on some **episode** in history, such as the Revolutionary War or the civil rights movement, are also part of this group.

What better **pastime** is there than settling into your favorite chair with a good book? You may decide that a thousand words are actually better than a picture.

Check the Meaning

Choose the correct meaning for the word in bold type. Fill in the circle next to the correct meaning.

1. If you **fascinate** people, you
   - Ⓐ put them to sleep.
   - Ⓑ hold their interest and attention.
   - Ⓒ make them hungry.
   - Ⓓ trick them.

2. A **magazine** is
   - Ⓐ the landing between the floors of a building.
   - Ⓑ a large sign.
   - Ⓒ reading material published weekly or monthly.
   - Ⓓ a woman's hat.

3. In a **museum**, you are likely to find
   - Ⓐ expensive objects on display.
   - Ⓑ people studying to become doctors.
   - Ⓒ tombs and memorials to the dead.
   - Ⓓ weight lifters.

4. Great **literature** is
   - Ⓐ a large pile of paper.
   - Ⓑ a cookbook.
   - Ⓒ recordings of classical music.
   - Ⓓ writing of lasting value.

5. An **amateur** storyteller is one who
   - Ⓐ makes up his or her own stories.
   - Ⓑ works for pleasure rather than as a profession.
   - Ⓒ passes on the wisdom of old age to young people.
   - Ⓓ tells stories about sports.

6. An **episode** is
   - Ⓐ one part of a larger story or time period.
   - Ⓑ the exact center.
   - Ⓒ something that spreads quickly and widely.
   - Ⓓ a familiar saying.

7. Something that is **ancient**
   - Ⓐ moves around the sun.
   - Ⓑ is very funny.
   - Ⓒ is very old.
   - Ⓓ cannot be trapped.

8. A **pastime** is
   - Ⓐ someone's life story.
   - Ⓑ a way in which people spend free time.
   - Ⓒ an ability to read quickly.
   - Ⓓ an old address.

9. A **proverb** is
   - Ⓐ a short saying one hears often.
   - Ⓑ a word from another language.
   - Ⓒ something taken on a long trip.
   - Ⓓ a student.

10. A **novel** is
    - Ⓐ something used for digging.
    - Ⓑ a beginner.
    - Ⓒ a very high number.
    - Ⓓ a long, made-up story.

11. A person who writes an **autobiography**
    - Ⓐ tells the story of his or her life.
    - Ⓑ explains the actions of someone in history.
    - Ⓒ makes up a story about gods and goddesses.
    - Ⓓ knows about cars.

12. An example of **fiction** is
    - Ⓐ the heat created by rubbing two things together.
    - Ⓑ a true story about something that happened.
    - Ⓒ an imaginary or made-up story.
    - Ⓓ an action or adventure story.

B Study the Spelling

Word List

amateur	proverb	fascinate	novel
episode	pastime	literature	magazine
fiction	ancient	museum	autobiography

Form a list word by matching the beginning of a word in the first column with its ending in the second column. Write the list word.

nov   tion   **1.** _____

an   azine   **2.** _____

pas   biography   **3.** _____

prov   el   **4.** _____

fic   sode   **5.** _____

epi   erb   **6.** _____

mag   cient   **7.** _____

auto   time   **8.** _____

Write the list word for each clue.

9. It begins with two consonants. _____

10. It begins like *angel* and ends like *proficient*. _____

11. It has four syllables and ends with *ure*. _____

12. It begins like *fasten* and ends like *hallucinate*. _____

13. It has six letters. Three of them are vowels. _____

14. This word comes first in alphabetical order. _____

Add the missing letters. Write a list word.

15. pas___im___ _____

16. amat___ ___r _____

17. fas___ ___nate _____

18. autobi___gr___phy _____

C Build Your Skills

Language Tutor

The English language takes parts of words from other languages to make new words. Parts of three Greek words were used to make the word *autobiography*.

$$auto + bio + graph = \text{autobiography}$$
$$\text{(self)} \quad \text{(life)} \quad \text{(to write)}$$

The meaning for each word part is given in parentheses. Combine the word parts to make an English word. Write the word, then tell what the word means.

1. *bio* (life) + *logy* (study) = _____

_____

2. *phono* (sound) + *graph* (write) = _____

_____

3. *auto* (self) + *mobile* (motion) = _____

_____

4. *tele* (distance) + *phone* (sound) = _____

_____

5. *micro* (small) + *phone* (sound) = _____

_____

6. *photo* (light) + *graph* (write) = _____

_____

7. *tele* (distance) + *graph* (write) = _____

_____

8. *mono* (one) + *gram* (letter) = _____

_____

9. *bi* (two) + *cycle* (circle) = _____

_____

10. *tele* (distance) + *scope* (watch) = _____

_____

Score: / 10

D Proofread and Write

Julio made a list of things he needed to get at the library. He made four spelling mistakes. Cross out the misspelled words. Write the correct spellings above them.

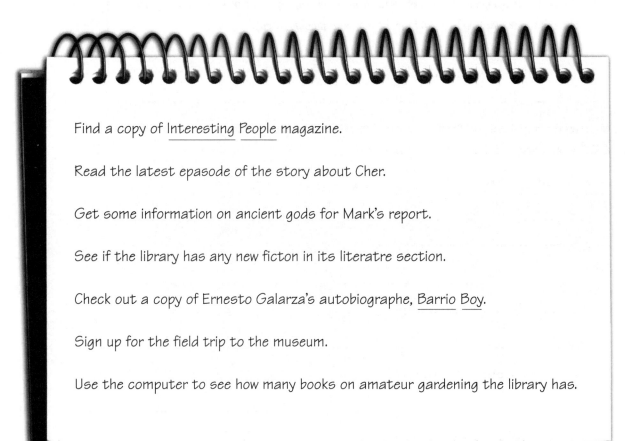

Find a copy of Interesting People magazine.

Read the latest epasode of the story about Cher.

Get some information on ancient gods for Mark's report.

See if the library has any new ficton in its literatre section.

Check out a copy of Ernesto Galarza's autobiographe, Barrio Boy.

Sign up for the field trip to the museum.

Use the computer to see how many books on amateur gardening the library has.

Writing Portfolio

Make a list of things you could do at your own library. Use another piece of paper. Use at least four list words.

Proofread your list carefully and correct any mistakes. Then make a clean copy and put it in your writing portfolio.

Never Too Old to Learn

Ⓐ Check the Meaning

Read the paragraph below. Think about the meaning of the words in bold type.

School is not just for children. It is a **valuable** resource for anyone at any age who wants to learn. Many cities and towns use their school buildings for adult classes in the evening. Here the adults who **reside** in the community can advance their education. You may be surprised by the number of courses offered. There are practical classes to teach the English language. Sometimes these classes are taught by **bilingual** instructors who also speak Spanish or some other language spoken in the community. Some classes teach people how to start their own businesses. Other classes are just for fun. Classes on playing cards, growing flowers, or collecting baseball cards are not unusual. To take advantage of these adult classes you may need to see an **advisor** at the school. He or she can tell you what classes are offered. The **attendance** may be limited to the first ten or twelve people who **enroll**. Find out what is available and sign up right away.

Choose the correct meaning for the word in bold type. Fill in the circle next to the correct meaning.

1. A **bilingual** instructor
- Ⓐ teaches many classes.
- Ⓑ has studied in a foreign country.
- Ⓒ can speak two languages.
- Ⓓ is often late for class.

2. The area where you **reside** is one you
- Ⓐ go through on your way to work.
- Ⓑ disapprove of.
- Ⓒ live in.
- Ⓓ speak out against.

3. To **enroll** is to
- Ⓐ enter into something.
- Ⓑ form into a circle.
- Ⓒ trap in a net.
- Ⓓ fold in half.

4. An **advisor**
- Ⓐ gives advice.
- Ⓑ supports a person in an election.
- Ⓒ is an expert on advertising.
- Ⓓ believes in fortunetellers.

5. If something is **valuable**, it
- Ⓐ is over one hundred years old.
- Ⓑ is empty.
- Ⓒ moves from place to place.
- Ⓓ has great worth.

6. The **attendance** at a meeting is the
- Ⓐ entertainment provided.
- Ⓑ number of people there.
- Ⓒ size of the crowd expected.
- Ⓓ person or persons who get it started.

Check the Meaning

Read the paragraph below about television and cable. Think about the meaning of the words in bold type.

Television was once called chewing gum for the mind. TV has long been considered just a **diversion** for one's eyes and ears. It allows one's brain to relax. That **sentiment** has changed somewhat since cable television has arrived. No longer are viewers restricted to three or four programs. Many viewers have **access** to fifty, or even a hundred, channels. Some channels specialize in movies. Others focus on history, and still others on the news, the weather, or world events. Some schools offer courses on cable TV for home study. Many communities **reserve** one cable channel for local needs. Such channels make it possible to **implement** the plan to include all citizens in meetings of their **municipal** government. People no longer have to travel to city hall to see the meetings there. Cable television brings the meetings to them. Of course, most of what people see on television still gives their brain a rest. Now, at least, there are some choices.

Choose the correct meaning for the word in bold type. Fill in the circle next to the correct meaning.

7. If you **reserve** something, you
- Ⓐ use it up.
- Ⓑ save it.
- Ⓒ tell others about it.
- Ⓓ destroy it.

8. A **diversion**
- Ⓐ provides a change.
- Ⓑ is money a bank pays to customers.
- Ⓒ breaks an object into small pieces.
- Ⓓ sends a signal a long distance.

9. If you **implement** a plan, you
- Ⓐ change it.
- Ⓑ turn it down.
- Ⓒ speak about it often.
- Ⓓ put it in motion.

10. A **sentiment** is a(n)
- Ⓐ guard.
- Ⓑ opinion or belief.
- Ⓒ person who cries frequently.
- Ⓓ pleasant conversation.

11. If you have **access** to something, you
- Ⓐ have the right to enter or be involved.
- Ⓑ know how it works.
- Ⓒ are unable to buy it.
- Ⓓ can measure it.

12. A **municipal** government is
- Ⓐ run by a dictator.
- Ⓑ appointed by the governor.
- Ⓒ concerned with a city or town.
- Ⓓ based on religious beliefs.

Score: 12

B Study the Spelling

Word List

enroll	reserve	reside	access
municipal	advisor	implement	diversion
sentiment	valuable	bilingual	attendance

Write the list word or words for each clue.

1. They end with *ment*. _____ _____

2. It begins with a word part that means "two." _____

3. The word *serve* is part of its spelling. _____

4. It is formed from the word *value*. _____

5. The word *pal* is part of its spelling. _____

6. It is formed from the word *attend*. _____

7. Add a suffix meaning "one who" to the word *advise* to make this word.

_____

8. The word *sent* is part of its spelling. _____

9. It has the *-ion* suffix. _____

10. The word *side* is part of its spelling. _____

Add the missing syllable. Write a list word.

11. _____roll _____

12. ac_____ _____

13. munic_____pal _____

14. valu_____ble _____

15. atten_____ _____

16. _____version _____

17. sent_____ment _____

18. advi_____ _____

C Build Your Skills

Language Tutor

Add *'s* to singular words to make them show ownership or possession. Add only an apostrophe (') to plural words that end in *s* to make them show ownership or possession.

Singular Possessive
the instructor's question

Plural Possessive
the students' answers

Rewrite each sentence. Change the underlined words to make them show ownership or possession. The first one has been done for you.

1. The <u>concerns of the viewers</u> were stated in the letter.

   The viewers' concerns were stated in the letter.

2. The <u>suggestion of the advisor</u> helped me make the decision.

   _____

3. English is taught in the <u>classroom of the school.</u>

   _____

4. The coach learned the <u>sentiment of the players.</u>

   _____

5. A meeting was held to explain the <u>benefits of the company.</u>

   _____

6. The <u>attendance of the employees</u> was required.

   _____

7. They listened to the <u>explanation by the plant manager.</u>

   _____

8. New equipment would improve the <u>safety of the workers.</u>

   _____

9. Maps would show the <u>location of the classroom.</u>

   _____

10. I heard the <u>report of the city counselors</u> on cable television.

    _____

Score: 10

D Proofread and Write

A cable television station received the following note. It has three spelling mistakes. It also has a mistake in the use of a possessive. Cross out each word with a mistake. Write the word correctly above it.

July 23, 1997

Station Manager

WCMP TV

721 Main St.

Fort Worth, TX 76109

Dear Station Manager:

Your cable programs are a valuable part of my day. I especially like your broadcasts of municiple events. Lately, though, my acess has been limited. I think the cable has been damaged by a squirrel. Several reside in a nearby tree. I think I found marks from the squirrel's teeth on the outside of the cable.

I need your companys help to fix this. Attendence at town meetings is difficult for me. I plan to enroll in a course that meets on Tuesday. This is the day most town meetings are held.

Thanks for your help.

Sincerely,

Becky Wren

Becky Wren

Writing Portfolio

Write a letter to a TV or radio station and comment on its programming. Use your own paper. Use at least four list words.

Proofread your letter carefully and correct any mistakes. Then make a clean copy to mail to the station or put in your writing portfolio.

15

Storm Warnings

Ⓐ Check the Meaning

Read the paragraphs below. Think about the meaning of the words in bold type.

It is true that everyone talks about the weather, but no one can do much about it. We may not be able to change the weather, but we can **forecast** it. As a result, we can be better prepared if bad weather comes our way. Nowadays the **frightening** possibility that a huge storm will catch us by surprise is quite remote.

The kind of weather problems people face depends largely on where they live. People in the southeastern United States must deal with the occasional **hurricane**. The wind and water in these storms can be very dangerous. Fortunately, the National Weather Service, the **organization** that keeps track of the weather, can usually tell where and when a hurricane will hit land. Like most severe weather, hurricanes are **seasonal** events. Most occur in August or September. Once spotted, they can be followed by planes or a weather **satellite** circling above the earth. If it appears that the storm will **imperil** a particular area, people can be advised to move inland.

People living in the Midwest can expect another type of weather **crisis**, the tornado. Like the hurricane, a tornado is a whirling mass of air. Tornadoes also occur at a certain time of year, in the spring. However, this is where the **parallel** ends. A tornado is far more difficult to **predict** than a hurricane. It is not possible to know exactly where a tornado's dark **column** will touch down. When certain conditions exist, a tornado watch will be announced. This means a tornado could be forming. If a tornado watch is changed to a tornado warning, it means a tornado has been seen. In either case, it is wise to seek shelter in a basement.

One good precaution is to have a **portable** radio. Electricity is often lost in a storm. With a battery-powered, portable radio a person can always hear the weather reports and know what to expect.

Check the Meaning

Choose the correct meaning for the word in bold type. Fill in the circle next to the correct meaning.

1. A **frightening** event
   - (A) creates fear.
   - (B) happened long ago.
   - (C) cannot be explained.
   - (D) involves animals.

2. The **parallel** of something
   - (A) is the same color.
   - (B) involves numbers.
   - (C) is used in athletic events.
   - (D) is like it in a number of ways.

3. If something is **portable**, it
   - (A) is free of dirt.
   - (B) can be moved about easily.
   - (C) is wrapped in paper.
   - (D) is soft to the touch.

4. To **forecast** is to
   - (A) drop into water.
   - (B) tell what will happen.
   - (C) harm.
   - (D) move forward slowly.

5. A **seasonal** event happens
   - (A) in secret.
   - (B) on the sea.
   - (C) in a specific season.
   - (D) with little planning.

6. If you **imperil** something, you
   - (A) decorate it.
   - (B) separate it.
   - (C) watch it for a long period of time.
   - (D) put it in danger.

7. A **column** is
   - (A) shaped like a long, narrow post.
   - (B) used to cut hair.
   - (C) part of a lock.
   - (D) a tool used in farming.

8. An **organization** is a
   - (A) type of cloth.
   - (B) business that repairs organs.
   - (C) group of people working together.
   - (D) vegetable stand.

9. If you **predict** something, you
   - (A) open it.
   - (B) say it is going to happen.
   - (C) refuse to accept it.
   - (D) carry it a long distance.

10. A **satellite**
    - (A) travels around a planet.
    - (B) is anything soaked in water.
    - (C) is a type of lamp.
    - (D) decays rapidly.

11. A **hurricane** is a
    - (A) type of sweet food.
    - (B) part of the body.
    - (C) tropical storm.
    - (D) believer in ancient religions.

12. A **crisis** is
    - (A) a foolish statement.
    - (B) an impossible task.
    - (C) a sudden danger.
    - (D) an early life form.

B Study the Spelling

Word List

organization	crisis	imperil	frightening
forecast	column	parallel	satellite
portable	hurricane	seasonal	predict

Write the list word or words for each clue.

1. It is formed from the word *season*. _____

2. It ends with a silent *n*. _____

3. They have a double *ll* in their spelling.

_____ _____

4. It is formed from the word *organize*. _____

5. It has a double *r* in its spelling. _____

6. It is formed from the word *fright*. _____

7. They begin with two consonants. _____

_____ _____

8. It begins like *impersonate* and ends like *evil*. _____

9. The word *cast* is part of its spelling. _____

10. The word *able* is part of its spelling. _____

Circle the list word in each of these longer words. Write the list word.

11. reorganization _____

12. imperiled _____

13. prediction _____

14. columnist _____

One word in each group is misspelled. Circle the misspelled word, then write it correctly.

15. predict   satelite   imperil   _____

16. huricane   column   portable   _____

17. organization   seasonal   parallell   _____

18. crisis   forecast   frightaning   _____

Score: 18

Ⓒ Build Your Skills

Language Tutor

Some words have "silent" letters. You do not hear these letters when you say the words. However, these letters are needed to spell the words.

colum<u>n</u>

Sometimes you can hear the silent letter in a related word. Thinking of this related word will give you a spelling clue.

colum<u>n</u>   colum<u>n</u>ist

Say each underlined word to yourself. Circle the silent letter in the word. Then write the word.

1. We need a <u>plumber</u> to fix the leak. _____

2. Do not throw the <u>wrapper</u> on the ground. _____

3. The dishes were kept in the <u>cupboard</u>. _____

4. His funeral was a <u>solemn</u> occasion. _____

5. I tried to <u>fasten</u> the line to the tree. _____

6. Chang had to <u>hustle</u> to work. _____

7. <u>Autumn</u> is my favorite time of year. _____

8. I love ice cream with <u>raspberries</u>. _____

9. The snow would <u>glisten</u> in the moonlight. _____

10. The story is about a poor <u>shepherd</u>. _____

Each pair of words below is related in meaning and spelling. Copy each pair. Then circle the letter that is heard in the first word but is silent in the second word.

11. limber   limb   _____

12. bombard   bomb   _____

13. crumble   crumb   _____

14. soft   soften   _____

15. moist   moisten   _____

16. signal   sign   _____

Score: ⬜ / 16

D Proofread and Write

The weather service sent this warning to people living near the shore. It made four spelling mistakes.
Cross out the misspelled words. Write the correct spellings above them.

TO: Everyone Living near the Shore

FROM: Your Weather Service

The seasonal risk of a huricane is high this year. Our experts believe there will be a

paralell between this year's storms and the worst year on record. Good organizashun

is needed in a crisis. The new satallite will help us predict these frightening storms.

Listen to reports on a portable radio. This will allow you to leave the area before the

crisis. Remember, these storms can also produce tornadoes. If you see a dark column

come down from a cloud, take cover under a bridge or in a basement.

Write some advice for people in a storm. Use at least four list words.

_____

_____

_____

_____

_____

_____

Writing Portfolio

Proofread your advice carefully and correct any mistakes. Then make a clean
copy and put it in your writing portfolio.

Getting Around

Ⓐ Check the Meaning

Read the paragraph below. Think about the meaning of the words in bold type.

When our country was just a **series** of villages and small towns, **mobility** was not a problem. Most people could walk to stores and to churches. Now getting to work or to the store means traveling long distances. Moreover, it means being part of a crowd of other people doing the same thing. Getting where we need to be often depends on finding an **appropriate** form of public **transportation**. In the larger cities, buses, subways, and trains are usually the fastest and least expensive **means** of getting around. However, the chances that a bus or subway takes a direct **route** from your home to your job are small. You may need to take several buses or trains. This means studying schedules and maps of each route carefully. Someone in the office of public transportation is usually available to help you. Do not be afraid to call.

Choose the correct meaning for the word in bold type. Fill in the circle next to the correct meaning.

1. Mobility is
- Ⓐ a body of water around a castle.
- Ⓑ the building of models.
- Ⓒ the ability to move about.
- Ⓓ a misunderstanding.

2. Someone who has the **means** to do something
- Ⓐ has what it takes to get it done.
- Ⓑ is unlikely to do it.
- Ⓒ talks about it often.
- Ⓓ can do it only when very angry.

3. Another word for **appropriate** is
- Ⓐ expensive.
- Ⓑ suitable.
- Ⓒ damaged.
- Ⓓ silly.

4. A **series** is
- Ⓐ a number of things in a row.
- Ⓑ a strongly built house.
- Ⓒ a type of medicine.
- Ⓓ the lowest part of a machine.

5. If you need **transportation**, you need
- Ⓐ a type of net.
- Ⓑ help with a difficult choice.
- Ⓒ the services of a doctor.
- Ⓓ a way to get someplace.

6. A **route** is
- Ⓐ the part of a plant that grows underground.
- Ⓑ a round shape.
- Ⓒ a path from one place to another.
- Ⓓ a place to rest.

Check the Meaning

Read the paragraphs below. Think about the meaning of the words in bold type.

Driving long distances on major U.S. highways has become easier in **recent** years. There are several reasons for this change. One is the placement of rest areas at regular **intervals**. They usually occur every thirty to fifty miles. At a rest area, you can expect to find a restroom **facility**, soft drink machines, and a place to relax and walk a dog. Whether taking a long trip or just an afternoon **excursion**, a rest stop is always welcome.

Another help for drivers is the use of easy-to-read signs. Large green signs mark upcoming highways and towns. Brown signs tell of interesting places you may wish to visit. Exits that lead to food, fuel, or lodging also appear often. In many cases, the **symbol** for the business offering these services appears on the sign. This makes it easier to know exactly what kinds of services are available. Being unable to read traffic signs quickly should no longer be an **obstacle** to travel.

Choose the correct meaning for the word in bold type. Fill in the circle next to the correct meaning.

7. If something is an **obstacle**, it
- Ⓐ makes a lot of noise.
- Ⓑ falls over easily.
- Ⓒ stands in the way.
- Ⓓ marks an important place.

8. An **interval** is
- Ⓐ a discussion with a possible employer.
- Ⓑ the ability to guess the future.
- Ⓒ the space between two things.
- Ⓓ the place where two roads cross.

9. An **excursion** is a
- Ⓐ trip.
- Ⓑ drink from a cup.
- Ⓒ nap.
- Ⓓ vacation.

10. A **symbol** is
- Ⓐ a musical instrument.
- Ⓑ something that stands for something else.
- Ⓒ a type of riddle.
- Ⓓ part of an engine.

11. A **facility**
- Ⓐ is a room where teachers meet.
- Ⓑ provides a service.
- Ⓒ is a make-believe story.
- Ⓓ is a failure.

12. A **recent** event
- Ⓐ marked the crowning of a king or queen.
- Ⓑ is one attended by many people.
- Ⓒ happened not too long ago.
- Ⓓ provides healthy snacks.

Score: 12

B Study the Spelling

Word List			
route	appropriate	mobility	transportation
recent	facility	symbol	obstacle
series	interval	means	excursion

Write *symbol, mobility, obstacle,* and *interval* in alphabetical order. Use dots between the syllables.

1. _____ **3.** _____

2. _____ **4.** _____

Write a list word or words for each clue.

5. They end with a vowel plus an *l*.

_____ _____

6. The word *cent* is part of its spelling. _____

7. There is a double consonant in its spelling. _____

8. They end with an *s*. _____ _____

9. It is formed from the word *mobile*. _____

10. They have five letters and one syllable.

_____ _____

11. It begins like *transfer* and ends like *deportation*. _____

12. It begins like *interactive* and ends like *carnival*. _____

13. These words have four syllables and rhyme.

_____ _____

14. The vowel in the first syllable is a *y*. _____

Add the missing letters. Write the list word.

15. obst___c___e _____

16. ap___ropri___te _____

17. r___ut___ _____

18. int___rv___l _____

Score: ⬜/18

Lesson 16: Getting Around (95)

C Build Your Skills

Language Tutor

A dictionary gives the pronunciation of each entry word. It uses special symbols that stand for the sounds. If a word has two or more syllables, the dictionary also shows which syllable is stressed. The stressed syllable is in bold type and has a small mark over it.

Word	Pronunciation
route	ro͞ot *or* rout
recent	**rē**′ sənt
obstacle	**ŏb**′ stə kəl
facility	fə **sĭl**′ ĭ tē

Study the complete list of sounds and symbols on page 146.

Study each pronunciation. Write the word that matches the pronunciation.

1. kŏm′ ĭk	color	comet	comic	_____
2. gĕst	guest	quick	guiz	_____
3. ŏb′ jĕkt	observe	open	object	_____
4. sîr′ ēz	service	series	serious	_____
5. mō′ tər	motor	mountain	mother	_____
6. āt	eight	at	apple	_____
7. ăt	add	ate	adapt	_____
8. roi′ əl	rubber	ruin	royal	_____
9. ûr′ bən	urban	under	upset	_____
10. jo͝or′ ē	journey	jury	glory	_____
11. fē′ chər	feature	future	feather	_____
12. fĭk′ shən	freckle	fidget	fiction	_____
13. sôs	sauce	sausage	saw	_____
14. ground	grouch	groom	ground	_____
15. pär′ sən	parson	pardon	parlor	_____

Score: 15

D Proofread and Write

Luis left these directions for Maria. He made four spelling mistakes. Cross out the misspelled words.
Write the correct spellings above them.

Maria,

The driver of my car pool must work late tomorrow. I need
transpertation home after work. Do you have the means to pick
me up? The best ruote is through the main part of town. It is
the most appropriate way to go this week because the repairs
on the other highway will be an obstacle. You will come to a series
of stop signs. They come at an interval of about a half mile.
Turn right at the third stop sign. You will see a sign with a big
lightbulb on it. That is the symbol for my company. I work in
the production facillity in the back. Please pick me up there.

Many thanks,
Luis

Write directions for getting someplace in your city or community. Use at least four list words.

_____

_____

_____

_____

_____

Writing Portfolio

Proofread your directions carefully and correct any mistakes. Then make a clean
copy and put it in your writing portfolio.

Unit 4 Review

Finish the Meaning

Fill in the circle next to the word that best completes each sentence.

1. The city promised to _____ a meal program for senior citizens.

   Ⓐ reserve   Ⓒ accumulate
   Ⓑ implement   Ⓓ encounter

2. The best way to deal with a _____ is to prevent it.

   Ⓐ colleague   Ⓒ crisis
   Ⓑ facility   Ⓓ guarantee

3. Hats and mittens are _____ clothing on cold, winter days.

   Ⓐ appropriate   Ⓒ infrequent
   Ⓑ frightening   Ⓓ mysterious

4. Some great works of _____ are not published until years after the author dies.

   Ⓐ attendance   Ⓒ convenience
   Ⓑ literature   Ⓓ appearance

5. The teenage years are often a difficult _____ in a person's life.

   Ⓐ means   Ⓒ exercise
   Ⓑ commitment   Ⓓ episode

6. Airplanes, trains, and other forms of transportation have greatly increased our _____.

   Ⓐ organization   Ⓒ mobility
   Ⓑ deficiency   Ⓓ priorities

7. A hobby like stamp collecting can be a worthwhile _____.

   Ⓐ advisor   Ⓒ procedure
   Ⓑ diversion   Ⓓ guardian

8. _____ athletes usually play just because they love the sport.

   Ⓐ Amateur   Ⓒ Recent
   Ⓑ Competitive   Ⓓ Professional

9. Carelessness with machinery can _____ everyone on the job.

   Ⓐ accommodate   Ⓒ predict
   Ⓑ encourage   Ⓓ imperil

10. The mayor is in charge of our _____ government.

    Ⓐ museum   Ⓒ municipal
    Ⓑ satellite   Ⓓ vocational

11. A small, _____ crib makes overnight trips to Grandma's house easy.

    Ⓐ portable   Ⓒ complicated
    Ⓑ valuable   Ⓓ permanent

12. The bikers stopped at _____ of twenty miles.

    Ⓐ series   Ⓒ assortments
    Ⓑ intervals   Ⓓ routines

Check the Spelling

Fill in the circle next to the word that is spelled correctly and best completes each sentence.

13. Things that happen today often seem to have a _____ in history.

Ⓐ parralel   Ⓒ paralell
Ⓑ parallel   Ⓓ parrallel

14. A child who hears two languages may grow up to be _____.

Ⓐ bilingual   Ⓒ bilinguel
Ⓑ biliengal   Ⓓ bilengual

15. The bald eagle is often used as a _____ for the United States.

Ⓐ simbol   Ⓒ symbol
Ⓑ cymbol   Ⓓ symble

16. Today, a visitor to Athens or Rome can still see parts of _____ buildings.

Ⓐ antient   Ⓒ anceint
Ⓑ ancent   Ⓓ ancient

17. A library card gives you _____ to thousands of books and other resources.

Ⓐ exces   Ⓒ acess
Ⓑ access   Ⓓ acces

18. A cardboard box can _____ a child for hours.

Ⓐ fasinate   Ⓒ fascinait
Ⓑ fascinate   Ⓓ facsinate

19. If you really want to achieve your goal, you can overcome any _____.

Ⓐ obstakel   Ⓒ obstacel
Ⓑ obstucle   Ⓓ obstacle

20. When adding a long _____ of figures, it is best to use a calculator.

Ⓐ colume   Ⓒ column
Ⓑ collumn   Ⓓ colemn

21. An election or opinion poll shows the _____ of the community.

Ⓐ sentiment   Ⓒ sentimint
Ⓑ centiment   Ⓓ sentament

22. Talking on the telephone is my favorite _____.

Ⓐ passtime   Ⓒ pastiem
Ⓑ pasttime   Ⓓ pastime

23. Every summer our family takes an _____ to the beach.

Ⓐ excurcion   Ⓒ ecskursion
Ⓑ excursion   Ⓓ excersion

24. Most sports are _____: football in the fall; baseball in the spring.

Ⓐ seesonal   Ⓒ seasunal
Ⓑ seasonal   Ⓓ seasonul

Score: _____ / 24

Income Tax

Ⓐ Check the Meaning

Read the paragraphs below. Think about the meaning of the words in bold type.

It is the job of the federal government to provide certain things for its citizens. A huge military force is maintained to protect them from enemies. In the event of a **disaster**, such as a flood or forest fire, victims can usually **borrow** money from the government to rebuild. Where does the government get its money? There is just one source: taxes. Taxes come in many forms. Airline tickets, tobacco, and goods coming into the country are taxed. However, the **primary** source of money is the tax on the earnings of each worker, the income tax.

The amount of income tax someone pays depends on how much he or she earns. An **estimate** of the tax one owes is withheld from each paycheck. Once a year everyone who has earned money must send the government a tax return. The return should give an **accurate** report of money earned and tax that has already been paid. If more has been taken from paychecks than a worker owes, he or she gets money back. If a taxpayer owes more money, he or she must send it with the tax return. It is important for a taxpayer to **disclose** all income. Employers must give each employee a form showing how much the worker earned and how much tax was taken out. Failure to **divulge** all income could result in a fine. On the other hand, the tax laws allow people to **exempt** some money from the income they report. A person supporting a child or another **dependent** may reduce the amount of income he or she reports. If you can **eliminate** certain money from the income you report, your taxes will be less.

The tax laws can be very **complex**. Many people are unable to **interpret** the instructions. The government provides free help for taxpayers. Several preparation services also offer help, but they charge fees.

Check the Meaning

Choose the correct meaning for the word in bold type. Fill in the circle next to the correct meaning.

1. If someone **divulges** a secret, he or she
   - (A) pays money to learn it.
   - (B) changes it to make it more interesting.
   - (C) tells it.
   - (D) cannot believe it.

2. The **primary** source of something is
   - (A) of little importance to anyone.
   - (B) its most important source.
   - (C) not well known.
   - (D) no longer available.

3. A **complex** law
   - (A) has many confusing details.
   - (B) regulates homes and other types of buildings.
   - (C) may be passed quickly without a vote.
   - (D) does not apply to citizens.

4. If you **exempt** something, you
   - (A) strongly dislike it.
   - (B) desire it.
   - (C) move it around.
   - (D) free it or excuse it.

5. An **estimate** is
   - (A) a large piece of land.
   - (B) a rough guess.
   - (C) an unclear set of directions.
   - (D) an official announcement.

6. If a report is **accurate**, it is
   - (A) correct and exact.
   - (B) very long.
   - (C) neatly prepared.
   - (D) colorful.

7. When people **interpret** something, they
   - (A) say bad things about it.
   - (B) defend it.
   - (C) explain it.
   - (D) put it on display.

8. A **disaster** is
   - (A) a loud disagreement.
   - (B) a meeting of important government workers.
   - (C) a flower that blooms in the fall.
   - (D) anything that causes a great deal of ruin.

9. When you **borrow** something, you
   - (A) use it and then return it.
   - (B) buy it.
   - (C) damage it.
   - (D) send it far away.

10. When people **disclose** something, they
    - (A) hide it.
    - (B) make it known to everyone.
    - (C) place it in a safe place.
    - (D) forget it.

11. A **dependent** is
    - (A) damage done to one's property.
    - (B) a type of jewelry worn around the neck.
    - (C) a deep hole.
    - (D) someone or something that needs help.

12. Another word for **eliminate** is
    - (A) remove.
    - (B) raise.
    - (C) believe.
    - (D) punish.

B Study the Spelling

Word List

interpret	estimate	complex	disaster
primary	accurate	divulge	borrow
disclose	eliminate	exempt	dependent

Circle the list word in each of these longer words. Write the word.

1. complexity _____

2. inaccurate _____

3. exemption _____

Write the list word or words for each clue.

4. They have a double consonant in their spelling.

_____ _____

5. It begins with two consonants. _____

6. They begin with the *dis-* prefix.

_____ _____

7. The word *close* is part of its spelling. _____

8. They end with *ate.* _____

_____ _____

9. Change one letter in *sorrow* to make this word. _____

Add the missing syllable. Write the list word.

10. esti_____ _____

11. _____empt _____

12. di_____ _____

One word in each group is misspelled. Circle the misspelled word, then write it correctly.

13. borrow   disclose   depandent   _____

14. interprat   exempt   accurate   _____

15. divulge   disaster   elimanate   _____

Score: 15

ⓒ Build Your Skills

Language Tutor

A prefix is a word part added to the beginning of a word or root. A root is a word part that has meaning, but cannot stand alone. The prefix adds meaning to the word or root.

The *ex-* prefix adds the meaning "out of" or "free from" to a word or a root.

<u>ex</u>empt	to free someone from a duty
<u>ex</u>claim	to shout out

Write the word from the box next to its meaning. Then write a sentence using the word.

expand	exhale	exclude	extinguish
exit	expire	explode	export

1. to breathe out _____

_____

2. to keep out; to prevent from entering _____

_____

3. to blow up or burst out _____

_____

4. to send out of the country _____

_____

5. the way out; the act of going out _____

_____

6. to put out something, such as a fire _____

_____

7. to spread out or enlarge _____

_____

8. to run out or come to an end, such as time in a game _____

_____

⒟ Proofread and Write

Kwan planned to get help with his taxes this year. He made an appointment with someone at the Internal Revenue Service, or IRS. He wrote these questions out so he would remember to ask them. Kwan made four spelling mistakes. Cross out the misspelled words. Write the correct spellings above them.

- How do you intrepret the rule on child-support payments? Can I eliminate the $200 a month I pay my ex-wife from my total income?

- I think my employer made a mistake on my W-2 form. I do not think the numbers are accerate. What should I do?

- Can I claim my mother as a dependent? I pay most of her bills. I estimate I spend $500 per month for her food and other expenses.

- I had to borrow money to buy my house. Is the interest I pay on this loan exampt from income tax?

- Is the information I give you kept secret or will you disclaze it to others?

Writing Portfolio

On another piece of paper, write some questions you have about taxes. Use at least four list words. Proofread your questions carefully and correct any mistakes. Then make a clean copy and put it in your writing portfolio.

The Jury System

Ⓐ Check the Meaning

Read the paragraphs below. Think about the meaning of the words in bold type.

In 1801, Thomas Jefferson, the third president of the United States, spoke of the key **principles** of democracy. One principle he stated was the right to a trial by a fair and **impartial** jury. This right to be judged by ordinary people is a **privilege** many in the world are denied. In some countries, one's guilt is decided by a few military officers or a judge. They may choose to ignore the evidence in deciding the outcome of the trial.

To make the jury system work, however, all citizens must do their share. From time to time, people are asked to serve on a jury. This service may **interfere** with a job or other plans. Nevertheless, it is **vital** that an honest effort be made to perform this duty. To get a fair trial, a **diversity** of people and ideas must be present on the jury. If only people with free time agree to serve, this will not happen. The jury system shows the faith we place in the common sense and fairness of every citizen.

Choose the correct meaning for the word in bold type. Fill in the circle next to the correct meaning.

1. If something is **vital**, it
  Ⓐ is practical.
  Ⓑ has great importance.
  Ⓒ is a danger to one's health.
  Ⓓ is easily seen.

2. Another word for **diversity** is
  Ⓐ foolishness.
  Ⓑ likeness.
  Ⓒ shortage.
  Ⓓ variety.

3. An **impartial** jury
  Ⓐ does not favor either side.
  Ⓑ is too small.
  Ⓒ takes too long to decide a case.
  Ⓓ is rude to the judge.

4. To **interfere** with something means to
  Ⓐ buy it.
  Ⓑ get in its way.
  Ⓒ scare it.
  Ⓓ replace it.

5. A **principle** is
  Ⓐ the person in charge of a school.
  Ⓑ a machine used in printing.
  Ⓒ a basic belief.
  Ⓓ any famous person from history.

6. A **privilege** is
  Ⓐ something with an unusual shape.
  Ⓑ the room where a jury meets.
  Ⓒ a special advantage some people have.
  Ⓓ an unwelcome gift.

Check the Meaning

Read the paragraphs below. Think about the meaning of the words in bold type.

The courts must decide many kinds of cases. The most familiar type of case is probably the criminal case. These cases decide whether someone has **violated** a law. If this person **proclaims** he or she is not guilty, the state is required to prove the charge. It does this by presenting the jury with any evidence it has. The accused can object to the use of some evidence. A judge must then **discriminate** between **valid** evidence and evidence that is unimportant or unfair. All witnesses are required to tell the truth. Failure to do so is **perjury**, a very serious crime.

Some court cases settle disagreements between people. For example, suppose a newspaper makes false or hateful statements about someone. Such statements could damage that person's reputation. He or she may charge the newspaper with **libel**. Was the newspaper wrong? Was it only practicing freedom of the press? These are difficult questions. Each side has the chance to state its case. In the end, however, the court must decide.

7. If something is **valid**, it is
(A) out of date.
(B) unknown to most people.
(C) very valuable.
(D) just and legal.

8. If you **proclaim** something, you
(A) take it by force.
(B) say it for everyone to hear.
(C) demand money for it.
(D) avoid it.

9. To **discriminate** is to
(A) tell one thing from another.
(B) prevent something from happening.
(C) deny the truth of a statement.
(D) explain in great detail.

10. Libel is the crime of
(A) missing a date in court.
(B) damaging the good name of a person or group.
(C) failing to prove a charge.
(D) lying to a judge.

11. Perjury is the crime of
(A) breaking a promise to tell the truth in court.
(B) punishing an innocent person.
(C) refusing to be on a jury.
(D) not listening to a witness.

12. People who **violate** something
(A) do not know about it.
(B) admire it.
(C) disregard or break it.
(D) cannot find it.

Score: 12

B Study the Spelling

Word List

vital	diversity	principle	discriminate
violate	libel	impartial	perjury
interfere	proclaim	privilege	valid

Write the list word or words for each clue.

1. It begins with the *im-* prefix and rhymes with *marshal*. _____

2. They have two syllables and five letters. _____

_____ _____

3. The word *claim* is part of its spelling. _____

4. It is formed from the word *diverse*. _____

5. They end with an *e*, a consonant, and another *e*.

_____ _____

6. It has three syllables. The middle syllable is the letter *o*.

_____

7. The word *jury* is part of its spelling. _____

8. They begin with the same two consonants. _____

_____ _____

Add the missing syllable. Write the list word.

9. princi_____ _____

10. in_____fere _____

11. vi_____ _____

12. li_____ _____

13. diver_____ty _____

14. _____jury _____

15. impar_____ _____

16. discrim_____ate _____

Score: ◻ / 16

C Build Your Skills

Language Tutor

Some words sound the same, but they do not have the same spelling or meaning.

Ms. O'Conner is the <u>principal</u> of my son's school.

His teacher explained the scientific <u>principle</u> of gravity.

Study the meaning of the underlined words in these sentences.

We need to <u>buy</u> some oil for the lawnmower.
The news was delivered <u>by</u> a messenger.

Frank ate the <u>whole</u> pizza by himself.
Please fix the <u>hole</u> in my shirt.

The visitors took pictures under the dome of the <u>capitol</u>.
The <u>capital</u> of Texas is Austin.

Not a <u>soul</u> was around when the game ended.
He is the <u>sole</u> support of his children.

Write each sentence. Add the correct word from within the parentheses.

1. What is the (capitol; capital) of Georgia?

_____

2. Democracy is based on the (principal; principle) of equality.

_____

3. I will be home the (whole; hole) evening.

_____

4. It is the finest stereo money can (by; buy).

_____

5. The child was the (soul; sole) survivor of the crash.

_____

Score: 5

D Proofread and Write

Hector was among several people being considered for a jury. Before he could be on the jury, he had to answer four questions. He made four spelling mistakes in his answers. Cross out the misspelled words. Write the correct spellings above them.

Do you promise to answer these questions honestly?

Yes, I will answer honestly. I know that perjary is a terrible crime.

Do you understand how a jury works?

I know the principal that a person must be proven guilty. His or her guilt must be shown using valid evidence.

Do you think you can perform the duties well?

I know it is vital that I remain imparsial. I cannot let my personal feelings intrefere with my work on the jury. I feel I can do this.

Do you promise to avoid discussing the case with anyone but the others on the jury?

I know I must think only of the evidence, not what others think. I will not violate this important rule.

Writing Portfolio

Copy the questions Hector was given and write your own answers to them. Use your own paper. Use at least four list words. Proofread your questions and answers carefully and correct any mistakes. Then make a clean copy and put it in your writing portfolio.

Running for Office

Ⓐ Check the Meaning

Read the paragraphs below. Think about the meaning of the words in bold type.

On election day, you have the right to vote for the candidate of your choice. Have you ever wondered how these people got their names on the ballot? There is no single answer. Running for an office in a small town may be rather simple. A **potential** candidate must live in the town or region the office serves. Then he or she must collect the signatures of the required number of voters on a **petition**. An official of the town will **verify** the signatures to be sure they are genuine. All candidates must complete this process by a certain date, usually months before the election. This **enables** the town clerk to print ballots in time for the election.

The process is more complicated when it comes to a state or national office. Running for these offices is a full-time job. Ordinarily, only experienced **politicians** seek these offices. Running for such important offices is also very costly. A candidate usually needs the support of a political party. A party is made up of people who **concur**, or agree, on most questions of government **policy**. Even so, differences between party members do occur. Arriving at a **consensus** on so many **issues** is often impossible. However, in the end, each party must choose just one candidate for each office. This choice is made at a large meeting called a convention. Perhaps hundreds of **delegates** will vote for the party's choice.

The delegates may argue bitterly for their choice. It may be hard, at times, to believe that everyone there shares the same political beliefs. Once a candidate gets the needed number of votes, the others usually **concede** defeat. As a show of unity, all delegates vote for the winner. This makes the victory **decisive**. Party members then try to put aside their differences and give all their support to the candidate.

Check the Meaning

Choose the correct meaning for the word in bold type. Fill in the circle next to the correct meaning.

1. An **issue** is
   - (A) a subject being argued or discussed.
   - (B) a three-sided figure.
   - (C) a sore spot on the skin.
   - (D) an area surrounded by water.

2. If a person **concedes** defeat, he or she
   - (A) denies it happened.
   - (B) demands an apology for it.
   - (C) admits it happened.
   - (D) decides to enjoy it.

3. Another word for **potential** is
   - (A) powerful.
   - (B) weak.
   - (C) lovable.
   - (D) possible.

4. A **petition** is a
   - (A) divider between rooms.
   - (B) paper asking for something.
   - (C) type of voting machine.
   - (D) religious service.

5. A **decisive** victory is
   - (A) confusing.
   - (B) firm and beyond doubt.
   - (C) one that requires a decision.
   - (D) kept secret from the voters.

6. To **enable** is to
   - (A) damage beyond repair.
   - (B) cover with a thick coat.
   - (C) surround with a type of wall.
   - (D) provide what is needed to do something.

7. Another word for **concur** is
   - (A) argue.
   - (B) discuss.
   - (C) agree.
   - (D) sleep.

8. A **policy** is a
   - (A) plan for action.
   - (B) school for police officers.
   - (C) meeting of office holders.
   - (D) short pause.

9. When people **verify** something, they
   - (A) clean it thoroughly.
   - (B) remove it from view.
   - (C) prove it to be true.
   - (D) change its shape.

10. A **delegate** is
    - (A) a place that serves sandwiches.
    - (B) an opening in a fence.
    - (C) the name of a political party.
    - (D) a person who represents others.

11. If a group of people reaches a **consensus**, it
    - (A) comes to a general agreement.
    - (B) decides to leave a meeting.
    - (C) breaks apart.
    - (D) turns on itself.

12. A **politician** is someone who
    - (A) has served in the military.
    - (B) has been convicted of a crime.
    - (C) is active in politics.
    - (D) cannot run for office.

B Study the Spelling

Word List

policy	consensus	verify	concede
issue	concur	enable	decisive
potential	petition	politician	delegate

Write the list word or words for each clue.

1. The letter *s* is used three times in its spelling. _____

2. It begins like *decide* and ends like *adhesive*. _____

3. There is a double consonant in its spelling. _____

4. It begins like *enclose* and ends like *table*. _____

5. It rhymes with *terrify*. _____

6. It is formed from the word *politics*. _____

7. They have two syllables. Both syllables begin with *c*.

_____   _____

8. Its last syllable is the word *gate*. _____

Four list words begins with the letter *p*. Write them in alphabetical order. Circle the word with four syllables.

9. _____   **11.** _____

10. _____   **12.** _____

Write the list words with two syllables. Use a dot between the syllables.

13. _____   **15.** _____

14. _____

Add the missing syllable. Write the list word.

16. pe_____tion _____

17. de_____sive _____

18. politi_____ _____

19. consen_____ _____

20. is_____ _____

Score: 20

C Build Your Skills

Prefixes add meaning to roots, word parts that have meaning but cannot stand alone.

The *con-* and *com-* prefixes add the meaning "together" or "with."

<u>con</u>cur   to agree with

<u>com</u>bine   to bring or come together

Write the word from the box next to its meaning. Then write a sentence using the word.

compile	contaminate	compress	connect
contract	confer	conjunction	conspire

1. to put together; to collect _____

_____

2. to discuss together _____

_____

3. a place where two things come together _____

_____

4. to link together _____

_____

5. to press together _____

_____

6. a written agreement with someone _____

_____

7. to mix with impure elements _____

_____

8. to touch or come together _____

_____

⒟ Proofread and Write

A newspaper ran this story on Willy Sims, a candidate for the school board. The paper made four spelling mistakes. Cross out the misspelled words. Write the correct spellings above them.

SIMS STATES VIEWS AT MEETING

At a recent meeting, candidate Sims stated he will change the school's policy of raising taxes every year. He does not feel others have addressed the isue. He does conced the school needs more money. He wants instead to patition the state for more financial aid. Giving him a decisive victory will send a message to every state politican.

Write a newspaper story about someone running for office. It can be a real or a made-up candidate. Use at least four list words.

_____

_____

_____

_____

_____

_____

_____

_____

Writing Portfolio

Proofread your newspaper story carefully and correct any mistakes. Then make a clean copy and put it in your writing portfolio.

The Opening of the West

Ⓐ Check the Meaning

Read the paragraph below. Think about the meaning of the words in bold type.

A huge steel arch rises from the bank of the Mississippi River in St. Louis, Missouri. Called the Gateway Arch, it **commemorates** the opening of the West. This spot was chosen because it was from here that two explorers, Meriwether Lewis and William Clark, began a **courageous** journey in 1804. The United States had recently purchased a large area of land from France. It was the job of Lewis and Clark to find out what this land was like. For two years they **traversed** the continent. They traveled over **fertile** land, tall mountains, and raging rivers. They kept a record of the **abundant** herds of buffalo and other game they saw. Examples of plants and rocks were sent back for study. Perhaps most important, Lewis and Clark made the first maps of the area. Without these **achievements**, the opening of the West could not have occurred.

Choose the correct meaning for the word in bold type. Fill in the circle next to the meaning.

1. If something is **abundant**, it
   - Ⓐ is hard to find.
   - Ⓑ runs slowly.
   - Ⓒ appears in great numbers.
   - Ⓓ touches the sky.

2. An **achievement** is
   - Ⓐ a remarkable act.
   - Ⓑ a terrible crime.
   - Ⓒ a funny statement.
   - Ⓓ someone you know.

3. When people **commemorate** something, they
   - Ⓐ bury it.
   - Ⓑ do it a second time.
   - Ⓒ write about it.
   - Ⓓ honor its memory.

4. Another word for **courageous** is
   - Ⓐ simple.
   - Ⓑ brave.
   - Ⓒ heavy.
   - Ⓓ stupid.

5. **Fertile** land
   - Ⓐ is reddish in color.
   - Ⓑ cannot be crossed.
   - Ⓒ is good for growing plants.
   - Ⓓ gets little rain.

6. To **traverse** is to
   - Ⓐ pray.
   - Ⓑ deny.
   - Ⓒ cross.
   - Ⓓ raise up.

Check the Meaning

To be successful in their travels, Lewis and Clark needed to trade with the native **inhabitants**. Their **budget** for the trip included things they could trade for horses, canoes, and food. However, no one on their **expedition** could speak a Native American language. Finding someone to translate for them was of the **utmost** importance. The solution came in the form of a young Shoshone* (shō shō′nē) woman named Sacajawea (săk′ ə jə wē′ ə). The wife of a white man, Sacajawea spoke both Shoshone and English. Sacajawea was able to **influence** the way the natives reacted to Lewis and Clark. Many Native Americans had learned not to trust the white man. When they saw Sacajawea, however, they decided to **tolerate** these strangers. Thanks to Sacajawea, the Native Americans traded for the horses and food the explorers so badly needed.

* a Native American people of the northwestern United States

Choose the correct meaning for the word in bold type. Fill in the circle next to the meaning.

7. An **inhabitant** is
Ⓐ someone who lives in a particular place.
Ⓑ a person who speaks several languages.
Ⓒ a land without water.
Ⓓ a person with a disability.

8. An **expedition** is
Ⓐ an unkind remark.
Ⓑ a trip for a special purpose.
Ⓒ a game played with a ball.
Ⓓ a war between bitter enemies.

9. Another word for **utmost** is
Ⓐ closest.
Ⓑ greatest.
Ⓒ strangest.
Ⓓ trickiest.

10. A **budget** is a
Ⓐ type of animal.
Ⓑ meal served on a large table.
Ⓒ plan for spending money.
Ⓓ small flower.

11. If you **tolerate** someone, you
Ⓐ look at the person carefully.
Ⓑ keep the person far away.
Ⓒ put the person in jail.
Ⓓ recognize and respect the person.

12. To **influence** someone is to
Ⓐ trick someone into doing something.
Ⓑ harm someone.
Ⓒ cause someone to change in some way.
Ⓓ move someone to another location.

Score: 12

B Study the Spelling

Word List

tolerate	abundant	inhabitant	expedition
achievement	influence	budget	commemorate
utmost	traverse	fertile	courageous

Write the list word or words for each clue.

1. They have two syllables. _____ _____

_____ _____

2. It has three syllables, and there is an *ie* in its spelling. _____

3. There are two *o*'s and two *u*'s in its spelling. _____

4. The word *habit* is part of its spelling. _____

5. There is a double consonant in its spelling. _____

6. They end with *ate*. _____ _____

7. They end with *ant*. _____ _____

8. It begins like *exhaust* and ends like *position*. _____

9. It begins like *influenza* and ends like *difference*. _____

10. The second syllable is the word *most*. _____

11. Add three letters to *verse* to form this word. _____

Write the list word that is related to each of these words.

12. achieve _____   **14.** abundance _____

13. courage _____   **15.** tolerant _____

Add the missing syllable. Write the list word.

16. fer_____ _____

17. ex_____dition _____

18. commem_____rate _____

C Build Your Skills

Language Tutor

A comma separates three or more items in a series. The items can be words or groups of words. The comma is placed after each item except the last one.

For two years Lewis and Clark traveled over <u>fertile land</u>,
<u>tall mountains</u>, and <u>raging rivers</u>.
     2   3   1

They <u>climbed mountains</u>, <u>floated on rivers</u>, and <u>rode through forests</u>.
       1   2   3

Write these sentences. Add commas where they are needed. Not all sentences will need commas.

1. The explorers saw buffalo geese and prairie dogs.

_____

2. Food and moccasins are two uses for buffalo hides.

_____

3. Sickness injury and boredom were some of the explorers' problems.

_____

4. The trails were narrow rocky and dangerous.

_____

5. Go to the store buy a new cap and pay for it with a check.

_____

6. I like my lemonade cold sweet and fresh.

_____

7. The mouse ran across the hall through the room and under the rug.

_____

8. They had to swim across or turn back.

_____

Score: 8

D Proofread and Write

On her first trip to the West, April made these notes to describe what she saw. She made three spelling mistakes. She also forgot two commas. Cross out the misspelled words. Write the correct spellings above them. Add the commas where they belong.

> My budget would not allow me to fly to the west coast. I am glad now that I drove instead. It let me see the abundent beauty of our country. My expedition took me across fertile farmland. Here couragous men and women risked their lives to build new homes. A marker showed where a battle was fought years ago. It was there to commemorate the soldiers Native Americans and settlers who died there. The things I learned on this drive will influance me for years to come.

Write a description of things you have seen on a trip. It can be a real trip or one you make up. Use at least four list words.

_____

_____

_____

_____

_____

_____

_____

Writing Portfolio

Proofread your description carefully and correct any mistakes. Then make a clean copy and put it in your writing portfolio.

Unit 5 Review

Finish the Meaning

Fill in the circle next to the word that best completes each sentence.

1. We grow big, healthy tomatoes on the _____ farmland near the river.

Ⓐ complex   Ⓒ fertile
Ⓑ duplicate   Ⓓ appealing

2. The library is the _____ source of information.

Ⓐ dependent   Ⓒ kindergarten
Ⓑ primary   Ⓓ personal

3. The person they arrested refused to _____ that he was the thief.

Ⓐ concede   Ⓒ tolerate
Ⓑ calculate   Ⓓ estimate

4. It is very hard to _____ between two colors in the dark.

Ⓐ negotiate   Ⓒ interpret
Ⓑ traverse   Ⓓ discriminate

5. Money and location are often factors that _____ a person's decision about a job.

Ⓐ violate   Ⓒ influence
Ⓑ monitor   Ⓓ imperil

6. The bus driver _____ that we will arrive in New York City by noon, but she is not certain.

Ⓐ estimates   Ⓒ admits
Ⓑ verifies   Ⓓ forgets

7. _____ people are sure about the choices they make.

Ⓐ Utmost   Ⓒ Vague
Ⓑ Competitive   Ⓓ Decisive

8. Any _____ juror must answer several questions.

Ⓐ vital   Ⓒ potential
Ⓑ portable   Ⓓ flexible

9. Groups such as schools and churches are _____ from most taxes.

Ⓐ exempt   Ⓒ disclosed
Ⓑ valid   Ⓓ priorities

10. A _____ of opinions was expressed at the meeting.

Ⓐ reserve   Ⓒ diversion
Ⓑ diversity   Ⓓ alternate

11. The fish were _____; we could see lots of them in the clear water.

Ⓐ fertile   Ⓒ vague
Ⓑ exempt   Ⓓ abundant

12. The witness was accused of committing _____ at the trial.

Ⓐ policy   Ⓒ perjury
Ⓑ resistance   Ⓓ injury

Check the Spelling

Fill in the circle next to the word that is spelled correctly and best completes each sentence.

13. Never _____ your credit card number to anyone.

   Ⓐ devulge   Ⓒ divulje
   Ⓑ divulge   Ⓓ divuldge

14. On Memorial Day we honor the _____ men and women who died for their country.

   Ⓐ courageous   Ⓒ courajus
   Ⓑ coreageous   Ⓓ couragous

15. You can lose your _____ to drive a car if you drive carelessly.

   Ⓐ privlege   Ⓒ privilege
   Ⓑ privalege   Ⓓ priviledge

16. Be sure your math is _____ when you balance your checkbook.

   Ⓐ acurrate   Ⓒ accurate
   Ⓑ accurete   Ⓓ acurate

17. The jurors must reach a _____ on a person's guilt or innocence.

   Ⓐ consensus   Ⓒ cunsensus
   Ⓑ concensus   Ⓓ concencus

18. The right to an _____ trial is a hallmark of democracy.

   Ⓐ impartul   Ⓒ impaertial
   Ⓑ inpartial   Ⓓ impartial

19. With each new _____, Scott set his goals even higher.

   Ⓐ achevement   Ⓒ acheavment
   Ⓑ achievement   Ⓓ achievmint

20. During childhood we learn important _____ like honesty and fairness.

   Ⓐ principles   Ⓒ princeples
   Ⓑ principels   Ⓓ prenciples

21. The election was won by an experienced _____.

   Ⓐ polatition   Ⓒ politician
   Ⓑ politition   Ⓓ polatitian

22. We may not be able to _____ all pollution, but we can try to control it.

   Ⓐ elimanate   Ⓒ eliminate
   Ⓑ eliminait   Ⓓ aliminate

23. We will _____ the birth of our country with a fireworks display.

   Ⓐ comemmorate   Ⓒ commemorait
   Ⓑ commemarate   Ⓓ commemorate

24. To get on the ballot, you need signatures on a _____.

   Ⓐ petition   Ⓒ patision
   Ⓑ pation   Ⓓ peticion

STOP

Score: ___ / 24

Reading the Right Way

A Check the Meaning

Read the paragraphs below. Think about the meaning of the words in bold type.

What makes a person successful in school or on the job? This question has **inspired** experts to do study after study. The answers they offer to this question are rarely the same. Some have the **impression** that successful people have better work habits. Others feel that education is more important. There is one **trait** successful people seem to have that all experts agree on, however. Successful people are good readers. That is, they understand more of what they read. It makes sense, then, to **imitate** their reading habits. Here are a few things you can do to be a successful reader:

1. Decide on the **objective** of the reading. A **popular** novel read for enjoyment can be covered quickly. Reading a chapter in a textbook, however, takes longer.

2. For textbooks and similar reading material, the next step is to **survey** the selection. Read all titles and section titles. Note any key terms that are underlined or in dark type. Look up any words that are unfamiliar. Having to stop and find the meanings as you read will **hinder** your understanding of the selection.

3. Read the first paragraph and the first sentence of each **succeeding** paragraph. If there is a summary, read it as well. Review any photographs or illustrations.

4. Try to **anticipate** what you will learn when you read the entire selection. Then, on a piece of paper, write down several questions you expect to be answered.

5. Now you are ready to read the selection. As you read, jot down any information that helps answer the questions you wrote. Note any new information you did not expect.

6. When you finish, ask yourself each question and answer it. Make a **genuine** effort to give complete answers. It is usually better to write out your answers. **Oral** responses do not demand the same careful thinking.

Check the Meaning

Choose the correct meaning for the word in bold type. Fill in the circle next to the correct meaning.

1. To **imitate** something is to
   - (A) get it started.
   - (B) use it as a model to copy.
   - (C) threaten to destroy it.
   - (D) tell others about it.

2. To **hinder** is to
   - (A) delay.
   - (B) speak out.
   - (C) send away.
   - (D) make known.

3. The opposite of **genuine** is
   - (A) expensive.
   - (B) honest.
   - (C) fake.
   - (D) stupid.

4. An **impression** is
   - (A) a rude remark.
   - (B) someone who acts without thinking.
   - (C) the desire to do better.
   - (D) a vague idea.

5. An **oral** response is one that is
   - (A) quick.
   - (B) unusual.
   - (C) careful.
   - (D) spoken.

6. To **inspire** is to
   - (A) prevent.
   - (B) frighten.
   - (C) cause to happen.
   - (D) send away.

7. The **succeeding** paragraph is the
   - (A) next one.
   - (B) most important one.
   - (C) last one in a book.
   - (D) longest one.

8. An **objective** is
   - (A) a legal term.
   - (B) something that gets in the way.
   - (C) a goal.
   - (D) the opposite of something.

9. A **trait** is
   - (A) something traded.
   - (B) a quality or feature.
   - (C) a weakness.
   - (D) a friend.

10. When people **survey** something, they
    - (A) look it over in a general way.
    - (B) surround it.
    - (C) move it from place to place.
    - (D) open it carefully.

11. A **popular** novel
    - (A) is very long.
    - (B) tells a true story.
    - (C) is enjoyed by many people.
    - (D) is difficult to understand.

12. Another word for **anticipate** is
    - (A) observe.
    - (B) hide.
    - (C) copy.
    - (D) predict.

B Study the Spelling

Word List

trait	survey	hinder	anticipate	popular	succeeding
oral	inspire	imitate	objective	genuine	impression

Circle the list word in each of these longer words. Write the list word.

1. inspired _____

2. impressionable _____

3. popularity _____

4. hindering _____

5. surveyor _____

6. orally _____

Write the list word or words for each clue.

7. It has a double consonant followed by a double vowel. _____

8. They begin with vowels and have two syllables.

_____ _____

9. It begins like *surrender* and ends like *convey*. _____

10. It begins with two consonants and has one syllable. _____

11. They end with *ate*. _____ _____

12. They begin with the *im-* prefix.

_____ _____

Write *genuine*, *anticipate*, and *objective* in alphabetical order. Use dots between the syllables.

13. _____

14. _____

15. _____

Form a list word by adding the missing syllable. Write the list word.

16. genu_____ _____

17. suc_____ing _____

18. hin_____ _____

Score: /18

© Build Your Skills

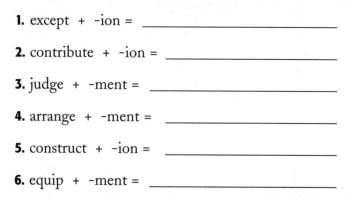

Language Tutor

A suffix is a word part added to the end of a word. The *-ion* and *-ment* suffixes change action words into naming words. Sometimes the spelling of a word changes when the suffix is added. For example, you usually drop the *e* before adding the suffix to action words that end in *e*.

Action Word		Suffix		Naming Word
impress	+	-ion	=	impression
imitate	+	-ion	=	imitation
argue	+	-ment	=	argument
entertain	+	-ment	=	entertainment

Change action words into naming words by adding the suffix.

1. except + -ion = _____

2. contribute + -ion = _____

3. judge + -ment = _____

4. arrange + -ment = _____

5. construct + -ion = _____

6. equip + -ment = _____

Write each sentence. Add the *-ion* or *-ment* suffix to the word in parentheses to make it a naming word.

7. Our manager's (encourage) helped us finish the work on time.

_____

8. The safety expert must complete her (inspect) of the machine.

_____

9. We plan to attend the (dedicate) of the memorial.

_____

10. This group works for the (prevent) of cruelty to animals.

_____

Score: _____ / 10

D Proofread and Write

Frank planned to read a chapter in his history textbook. He reviewed titles and key words in the chapter. Then he read the first paragraph. Frank wrote down these questions that he expected to answer when he read the chapter. He made four spelling mistakes. Cross out the misspelled words. Write the correct spellings above them.

What could inspire so many people to come to the United States in the 1880s?

Was it their objective to get better jobs?

Did the government anticapate so many people wanting to come into the United States?

Did as many people arrive in succeding years?

What was their first impresion of this country?

Did their inability to speak English hinder them?

Did they receive a genuin welcome from the citizens of the United States?

Writing Portfolio

Choose a chapter in a book. Review any titles, key words, and illustrations. Then, on another piece of paper, write some questions you think the chapter will answer. Use at least four list words.

Proofread your questions carefully and correct any mistakes. Then make a clean copy and put it in your writing portfolio.

Keeping Track of Your Money

A Check the Meaning

Read the paragraph below. Think about the meaning of the words in bold type.

You are running short of cash, and payday is not for another week. It is **crucial** that you have money for gas to get to work. If this story sounds familiar, you need to make a budget. Properly used, a budget **indicates** if you will run out of money before payday. Here is how it works: Divide your monthly expenses into groups. Then add up the expenses in each group. The **criteria** for one group should be **essential** expenses that you cannot control, such as rent or a car payment. A second group could be important expenses, but ones in which a **reduction** is possible. Food is an example. Another group is expenses that could be eliminated. A **luxury** such as a movie belongs here. Make a final group for emergency expenses like car repairs. The total amount of all the groups cannot be more than your earnings. If it is, you must cut back until your budget matches your income.

Choose the correct meaning for the word in bold type. Fill in the circle next to the correct meaning.

1. If something is **crucial**, it
Ⓐ makes people laugh.
Ⓑ costs a great deal of money.
Ⓒ is extremely important.
Ⓓ is cruel.

2. A **luxury** is something
Ⓐ unnecessary but nice.
Ⓑ frightening.
Ⓒ giving off light.
Ⓓ done on a date.

3. To **indicate** something is to
Ⓐ demand it.
Ⓑ prevent it from happening.
Ⓒ place something over it.
Ⓓ point it out.

4. Another word for **essential** is
Ⓐ silly.
Ⓑ evil.
Ⓒ required.
Ⓓ small.

5. If there is a **reduction**, something
Ⓐ becomes smaller.
Ⓑ disappears.
Ⓒ explodes.
Ⓓ grows very large.

6. **Criteria** are
Ⓐ things that make people cry.
Ⓑ standards for judging.
Ⓒ germs.
Ⓓ lengthy reports.

Check the Meaning

Read the paragraph below. Think about the meaning of the words in bold type.

Having a budget is of no value if you do not use it. To follow your budget, keep a careful record of each dollar you spend every day. Keeping track of large bills, such as the rent, is easy. It is the small expenses—magazines, soft drinks, or lottery tickets—that are forgotten. These can add up and quickly **overwhelm** your budget. List each expense in its proper category. Add up the expenses you **incur** in each category. Do this regularly throughout each month. Ask yourself: Am I spending money too fast? In other words, can I stay within my budget? If you see a problem early enough, you can **modify** your spending habits. If you are going over your budget in a category, review how you spent the money. If you cannot **justify** the expense, eliminate it. It is always **preferable** to take action early. At the end of the month, you may not have many choices. You may once again have to face the **dilemma** of buying either gas or food, but not both.

Choose the correct meaning for the word in bold type. Fill in the circle next to the correct meaning.

7. To **incur** an expense is to
- Ⓐ disregard it.
- Ⓑ acquire it.
- Ⓒ pay it.
- Ⓓ challenge it.

8. A **dilemma** is
- Ⓐ a small animal.
- Ⓑ something damaged.
- Ⓒ a celebration.
- Ⓓ a difficult choice.

9. To **overwhelm** is to
- Ⓐ tame.
- Ⓑ overpower.
- Ⓒ float.
- Ⓓ overlook.

10. When people **modify** something, they
- Ⓐ change it.
- Ⓑ replace it.
- Ⓒ melt it.
- Ⓓ moisten it with water.

11. To **justify** an expense is to
- Ⓐ refuse to pay it because it is unfair.
- Ⓑ cut it in half.
- Ⓒ prove it to be proper.
- Ⓓ promise to pay it in the future.

12. If one thing is **preferable** to another, it is
- Ⓐ much larger.
- Ⓑ more desirable.
- Ⓒ less important.
- Ⓓ ahead of it in a line.

Score: 12

Ⓑ Study the Spelling

Word List

| crucial | modify | reduction | justify | indicate | preferable |
| essential | incur | dilemma | luxury | criteria | overwhelm |

Write the list word or words for each clue.

1. They end with *ify*. _____ _____

2. It is formed from the word *reduce*. _____

3. They have a double consonant in their spelling.

_____ _____

4. It has a silent *h* in its spelling. _____

5. They begin with the *in-* prefix.

_____ _____

6. It has four syllables and the last syllable has just one letter.

_____

7. It is formed from the word *crux*. _____

8. There are two *u*'s in its spelling. _____

9. It is formed from the word *prefer*. _____

10. It comes next after *dilemma* in alphabetical order. _____

Form a list word by matching the beginning of a word in the first column with its ending in the second column. Write the list word.

reduc	cur	**11.** _____
mod	ury	**12.** _____
cri	cial	**13.** _____
in	teria	**14.** _____
cru	tion	**15.** _____
lux	ify	**16.** _____

Score: /16

C Build Your Skills

Language Tutor

The suffix **-able** adds the meaning "able" or "worthy of" to a word. A final **e** in a word is usually dropped when adding the **-able** prefix.

prefer + -able = preferable, worthy of being preferred

Extra pay is preferable to less.

value + -able = valuable, having value

She owns a lot of valuable jewelry.

manage + -able = manageable, able to be managed

A group of four toddlers is manageable; a group of forty isn't.

Add the -able suffix to the word in parentheses. Write the sentence.

1. Be sure the clothes you buy are (wash).

_____

2. I took a very (enjoy) trip to the beach.

_____

3. The road was full of holes, but it was (pass).

_____

4. The machine was no longer (work).

_____

5. It is (advise) to see a dentist twice a year.

_____

6. Make yourself (comfort) in your favorite chair.

_____

7. Donate any (use) furniture to the church.

_____

8. Loud talking is not (accept) in the library.

_____

Score: 8

⒟ Proofread and Write

Debra kept a diary of how and where she spent money each day. She also made a few notes to help her with her budget. She made four spelling mistakes in her diary. Cross out the misspelled words. Write the correct spellings above them.

Saturday, February 8

I tried to modify my habit of buying coffee at work. Instead I made coffee at home and took it to work. I spent $1.50 for a doughnut, however. This is a luxery I can cut if I go over budget.

Lunch cost me $4.00 today. I think this is an essential expense. I seem to incer more food expenses now that I have quit smoking. I am still saving money. At almost $3.00 a pack, smoking was about to overwhelm my budget.

Buying a weekly bus pass is preferrable to paying the daily fare. It costs $12.00, but this is easy to justify. I will save $3.50 every week.

I stopped at the store and bought some clothes on sale. They cost $15.00. This is a reduction of $5.00 from the usual price. It is crusial that I spend no more money on clothes this month.

Writing Portfolio

Recall how you have spent money in the last few days. On another piece of paper, make some notes on how and when you spent the money. Use at least four list words.

Proofread your notes carefully and correct any mistakes. Then make a clean copy and put it in your writing portfolio.

23 Taking Notes

Ⓐ Check the Meaning

Read the paragraphs below. Think about the meaning of the words in bold type.

The human memory is remarkable, but it does have its limits. In fact, experts say that the ordinary person will recall less than ten percent of what he or she hears. This is hardly **adequate** in school or on the job. There are many good ways to improve your memory, however. One way is by learning how to take good notes. Good notes **condense** a teacher's lesson or a supervisor's instructions into a few, well-chosen words. These words then help you recall the entire message. Notes can give you an important **advantage** when getting ready for a test. Learning to take good notes is not something you can **accomplish** overnight. It takes practice. There are some things you can do.

Basic to good note taking is the ability to focus on the message. Do not let thoughts of last night's ball game or tomorrow's work **distract** you. People speak faster than you can write, so you cannot write down everything. Instead, learn to **distinguish** essential information from less important details. Write only the key information and **omit** the rest. Be alert to certain signals. Sometimes a teacher will say, "There are three things to remember." Immediately number your paper from 1 to 3 and be ready to write.

Whenever possible, **simplify** the language. It is not necessary to write complete sentences. Use words or phrases if possible. It is also more **efficient** to use abbreviations for long words. Take care, however, to be **consistent** in their use. The meaning may seem quite **evident** to you when you write the notes. Days later the abbreviation may be a mystery. Finally, review your notes immediately. **Clarify** anything you do not understand while it is still fresh in your mind. Ask questions, if necessary, to fill in any parts that you do not understand.

Check the Meaning

Choose the correct meaning for the word in bold type. Fill in the circle next to the correct meaning.

1. To **distinguish** between two things is to
   A) put one ahead of the other.
   B) see their differences.
   C) place a wall between them.
   D) destroy one of them.

2. If things **distract** you, they
   A) push you somewhere you don't want to go.
   B) injure you.
   C) take your attention away from something else.
   D) cause you great pain.

3. An **efficient** worker is one who
   A) is frequently late.
   B) wastes no time.
   C) dislikes other workers.
   D) is highly paid.

4. Another word for **adequate** is
   A) sticky.
   B) attractive.
   C) modern.
   D) satisfactory.

5. To **simplify** is to
   A) make easier.
   B) place in rows.
   C) increase in size.
   D) repair.

6. If someone is **consistent**, he or she is
   A) lazy and wasteful.
   B) rude and boring.
   C) regular and steady.
   D) proud and hard working.

7. If something is **evident**, it is
   A) used in a jury trial.
   B) easily seen.
   C) used in religious gatherings.
   D) uneven.

8. To **condense** is to
   A) confess.
   B) object to something.
   C) lead away.
   D) make shorter.

9. An **advantage** is
   A) an announcement.
   B) a person who works for you.
   C) a book of facts.
   D) a favorable position.

10. When people **accomplish** a job, they
    A) carry it out.
    B) give it to others to do.
    C) explain it to someone.
    D) compete for it.

11. To **omit** something is to
    A) decorate it.
    B) place it on top of something else.
    C) leave it out.
    D) empty it.

12. To **clarify** is to
    A) divide into parts.
    B) make understandable.
    C) turn into a liquid.
    D) listen carefully.

B Study the Spelling

Word List

simplify	distract	clarify	adequate	consistent	advantage
evident	efficient	omit	condense	distinguish	accomplish

Write the list word or words for each clue.

1. They end with *ent*. _____ _____

   _____

2. They have a double consonant in their spelling.

   _____ _____

3. They end with *ify*. _____ _____

4. It begins with *dis-* and has two syllables. _____

5. The word *sting* is part of its spelling. _____

6. It has two syllables. The first syllable has one letter. _____

7. They begin with *ad-*. _____ _____

8. They begin with *con-*. _____ _____

Circle the list word within each word. Write the list word.

9. inadequate _____

10. advantageous _____

11. accomplishment _____

12. distraction _____

Form a list word by adding the missing syllable. Write the list word.

13. con_____ _____

14. distin_____ _____

15. clari_____ _____

16. sim_____fy _____

17. ev_____dent _____

18. o_____ _____

Score: ⟋ 18

C Build Your Skills

Language Tutor

To simplify the names of the fifty states, the U.S. Postal Service uses two-letter abbreviations. Both letters are capitalized. Here are some examples:

AL	IL	NC	OH
AR	KS	NE	OR
AZ	MA	NH	TN
CA	ME	NJ	TX
CO	MN	NV	WA
IA	MS	NY	WV

Write the abbreviation from the box next to the name of the state it represents. The first one is done for you.

IL   **1.** Illinois

_____ **2.** New Hampshire

_____ **3.** Nevada

_____ **4.** North Carolina

_____ **5.** Ohio

_____ **6.** Alabama

_____ **7.** Oregon

_____ **8.** New Jersey

_____ **9.** Texas

_____ **10.** Arizona

_____ **11.** Arkansas

_____ **12.** Minnesota

_____ **13.** Colorado

_____ **14.** Iowa

_____ **15.** Massachusetts

_____ **16.** Nebraska

_____ **17.** Mississippi

_____ **18.** Kansas

_____ **19.** Tennessee

_____ **20.** West Virginia

_____ **21.** California

_____ **22.** New York

_____ **23.** Washington

_____ **24.** Maine

Score: _____ / 24

D Proofread and Write

Walter took these notes during a training course at work. He also wrote some questions about things he did not understand. He made four spelling mistakes. Cross out the misspelled words. Write the correct spellings above them.

Training Course Notes

Take adequate number of spare parts to job site.

If it's evadent you cannot acomplish the job, tell customer right away.

Be efficient. Don't let customer distrak you. But always be polite.

Clean and reuse any parts that still work. Show customer that you will omit that cost from the bill.

Questions

Can you please clarafy how to get new parts quickly?

How can I distinguish between a new and old model furnace?

Writing Portfolio

Choose a chapter to read in a textbook. Make some notes as you read. Then write some questions about things you still want to know. Use your own paper. Use at least four list words.

Proofread your notes and questions carefully and correct any mistakes. Then make a clean copy and put it in your writing portfolio.

Solving Problems

(A) Check the Meaning

Read the paragraph below. Think about the meaning of the words in bold type.

Problems come in all shapes and sizes. The **majority** of them can be solved by following certain steps. First, **evaluate** the situation and state the problem clearly. Do not let some **bias** confuse you. For example, do not tell your co-workers that your boss is a jerk. Instead, face the problem: you don't know how to get along with your boss. Next, list as many solutions as possible. Do not list just the **logical** solutions. Include all of your ideas, no matter how strange or **unconventional**. You might talk to the boss about the problem, do an extra job for her, or **compliment** her on the great job she is doing. Explore each solution. Then choose the best solution and think through the likely results. Finally, try it to see if it works. If the solution fails, you can always try another one.

Choose the correct meaning for the word in bold type. Fill in the circle next to the correct meaning.

1. To **compliment** someone is to
   - (A) praise someone for something.
   - (B) say things behind someone's back.
   - (C) refuse to believe someone.
   - (D) ask someone to leave.

2. A **logical** solution is one that is
   - (A) funny.
   - (B) too difficult to carry out.
   - (C) suggested by a friend.
   - (D) thoughtful and reasonable.

3. A **majority** of something is
   - (A) a small amount.
   - (B) the easy part.
   - (C) more than half.
   - (D) the part most easily seen.

4. To **evaluate** something is to
   - (A) send it away quickly.
   - (B) figure out its importance.
   - (C) make it level or even.
   - (D) break it into parts.

5. People who have a **bias** have
   - (A) several wives.
   - (B) a preference that prevents fair judgement.
   - (C) well-developed muscles.
   - (D) a talent for singing.

6. An **unconventional** solution is one that
   - (A) destroys natural resources.
   - (B) makes use of new information.
   - (C) is not normally considered.
   - (D) everyone likes.

Check the Meaning

Read the paragraph below. Think about the meaning of the words in bold type.

A report is due tomorrow, and you are staring at a blank piece of paper. Before you can **commence** writing, you need some ideas. Sometimes getting a few words on paper will be enough to **generate** a flood of ideas. One way to do this is called freewriting. Just start writing whatever comes to mind. Do not let concerns for spelling or punctuation **inhibit** you. Keep your pen moving for two or three minutes. Another technique is called clustering. Write your topic and circle it. Then write something you **associate** with the topic. If the topic is a computer, you might write "printer" or "software." Circle each related idea and connect it to the **initial** topic with a line. Brainstorming, a third technique, is like clustering. However, with brainstorming, an unlimited number of **dissimilar** ideas may be listed.

Choose the correct meaning for the word in bold type. Fill in the circle next to the correct meaning.

7. Another word for **initial** is
- (A) forgotten.
- (B) simple.
- (C) first.
- (D) difficult.

8. To **generate** is to
- (A) divide.
- (B) produce.
- (C) throw away.
- (D) move from place to place.

9. If things **inhibit** you, they
- (A) make you look foolish.
- (B) entertain you.
- (C) press against you.
- (D) hold you back.

10. Another word for **commence** is
- (A) begin.
- (B) delay.
- (C) repair.
- (D) buy.

11. **Dissimilar** ideas are
- (A) creative.
- (B) not alike.
- (C) unimportant.
- (D) difficult to explain.

12. To **associate** two things is to
- (A) deny they exist.
- (B) help them.
- (C) put them in alphabetical order.
- (D) bring them together in your mind.

B Study the Spelling

Word List

generate	commence	inhibit	evaluate	logical	unconventional
majority	dissimilar	initial	bias	associate	compliment

Write the list word or words for each clue.

1. They have a double consonant in their spelling. _____

_____   _____

2. It has four letters and two syllables. _____

3. It is formed from the word *logic*. _____

4. The word *major* is part of its spelling. _____

5. They end with *ate*. _____   _____

_____

6. They begin with the *in-* prefix. _____

_____

7. A prefix was added to *similar* to make this word. _____

8. They end with *al*. _____

_____   _____

9. It begins like *compose* and ends like *statement*. _____

10. They begin with the *com-* prefix.

_____   _____

Form a list word by adding the missing syllables. Write the list word.

11. un_____ven_____al   _____

12. major_____   _____

13. _____er_____   _____

14. _____val_____ate   _____

15. bi_____   _____

16. in_____it   _____

16

ⓒ Build Your Skills

Language Tutor

When you write a letter or address an envelope, you can abbreviate the terms for streets and roadways. Abbreviations make long words shorter and easier to read.

avenue	Ave.	road	Rd.	lane	La. or Ln.
boulevard	Blvd.	square	Sq.	terrace	Terr.
place	Pl.	highway	Hwy.	parkway	Pkwy.
court	Ct.	Street	St.	drive	Dr.
plaza	Plz.	trail	Tr.		

Write the following addresses. Use abbreviations for streets, roadways, and states. Refer to page 135 if necessary.

1. 395 Oxford Boulevard

Bloomington, Illinois 61701 _____

_____

2. 908 Acorn Plaza

Haverhill, Massachusetts 01832 _____

_____

3. 12 Spring Gardens Avenue

Waterloo, Iowa 50722 _____

_____

4. 4532 Backer Square

Fresno, California 93740 _____

_____

5. 1936 Five Oaks Drive

Durham, North Carolina 27707 _____

_____

6. 328 Biscayne Trail

Seattle, Washington 98124 _____

_____

7. 932 William Tell Parkway

Gulfport, Mississippi 39503 _____

_____

8. 1919 Tanglewood Terrace

Escondido, California 92033 _____

Score: 8

Ⓓ Proofread and Write

Harriet wrote this letter to the adult education director of her school. She used abbreviations for addresses. She made four spelling mistakes. Cross out the misspelled words. Write the correct spellings above them.

399 Central Ave.
Mobile, AL 36609
July 9, 1997

Dr. Lester Adams
Davis Community College
644 Genoa Sta.
Mobile, AL 36617

Dear Dr. Adams:

I am writing to find out if you plan to offer a course on report writing. The majoraty of the writing courses seem to be about grammar. My problem is writing logical, organized reports and trying to genarate good suggestions. A course where a teacher has time to evaluate the reports I write on the job would be the best.

I know classes commence in two weeks, so time is short. I have heard so many complements on your school. Your unconventionel approach to teaching seems to be very popular. I hope you have something that will help me.

Sincerely,

Harriet Washington

Harriet Washington

Writing Portfolio

Write a letter to a school or business. Use your own paper. Ask for information on something the school or business offers. Use the abbreviations for addresses, and use at least four list words.

Proofread your letter carefully and correct any mistakes. Then make a clean copy and put it in your writing portfolio.

Unit 6 Review

Finish the Meaning

Fill in the circle next to the word that best completes each sentence.

1. Hard work and study are two _____ for success.

   Ⓐ impressions   Ⓒ criteria
   Ⓑ facilities   Ⓓ signatures

2. A budget will help you _____ your expenses.

   Ⓐ celebrate   Ⓒ omit
   Ⓑ tolerate   Ⓓ anticipate

3. Sometimes a common problem will have a solution that is_____.

   Ⓐ unconventional   Ⓒ valuable
   Ⓑ courageous   Ⓓ dissimilar

4. The tax office will _____ any instructions you do not understand.

   Ⓐ hinder   Ⓒ verify
   Ⓑ clarify   Ⓓ imperil

5. Judges must be fair; they cannot show a _____ for either side in a case.

   Ⓐ solution   Ⓒ bias
   Ⓑ reduction   Ⓓ debit

6. If you forget an _____ part of the recipe, the dish will taste odd.

   Ⓐ evident   Ⓒ itemized
   Ⓑ essential   Ⓓ accurate

7. Children often _____ their parents' habits, both good and bad.

   Ⓐ violate   Ⓒ alternate
   Ⓑ imitate   Ⓓ calculate

8. The river is low because we did not get an _____ amount of rain this year.

   Ⓐ adjustable   Ⓒ oral
   Ⓑ initial   Ⓓ adequate

9. Poor study habits can _____ your progress in school.

   Ⓐ inhibit   Ⓒ pursue
   Ⓑ distract   Ⓓ exploit

10. Any task is easier if you have a clear and reasonable _____.

    Ⓐ pastime   Ⓒ advantage
    Ⓑ majority   Ⓓ objective

11. Only an expert can _____ between a real gem and a fake.

    Ⓐ perceive   Ⓒ distinguish
    Ⓑ distract   Ⓓ proclaim

12. If the weather is bad, we will have to _____ our vacation plans.

    Ⓐ redeem   Ⓒ pursue
    Ⓑ modify   Ⓓ authorize

Check the Spelling

Choose the word that is spelled correctly and best completes each sentence.

13. She faced the _____ of skipping lunch or being late for work.

    Ⓐ dilema   Ⓒ dilemma
    Ⓑ dillema   Ⓓ dillemma

14. Everyone needs a _____ on his or her work from time to time.

    Ⓐ compliment   Ⓒ complimint
    Ⓑ complament   Ⓓ complement

15. The team hopes to improve its standing with each _____ game.

    Ⓐ suceeding   Ⓒ succedding
    Ⓑ succeding   Ⓓ succeeding

16. Jeff is _____: He gets to work ten minutes early every day.

    Ⓐ consistint   Ⓒ cunsistent
    Ⓑ consistant   Ⓓ consistent

17. The best way to _____ your goals is to have a plan.

    Ⓐ acommplish   Ⓒ accommplish
    Ⓑ accomplish   Ⓓ accomplesh

18. One can usually tell if an apology is _____.

    Ⓐ jenuine   Ⓒ genuine
    Ⓑ genuien   Ⓓ genuene

19. Americans _____ the Fourth of July with fireworks and barbecues.

    Ⓐ associate   Ⓒ asocciate
    Ⓑ assosiate   Ⓓ associait

20. If you cannot _____ the expense, do not spend the money.

    Ⓐ justify   Ⓒ justafie
    Ⓑ justifie   Ⓓ justafy

21. Simple carelessness can _____ serious mistakes.

    Ⓐ genarate   Ⓒ jenarate
    Ⓑ generait   Ⓓ generate

22. An _____ worker gets the job done on time.

    Ⓐ eficcient   Ⓒ efficient
    Ⓑ efficcient   Ⓓ efficent

23. The audience became quiet at the _____ point in the movie.

    Ⓐ krucial   Ⓒ crusial
    Ⓑ crucial   Ⓓ crushul

24. We often try to copy the _____ of people we admire.

    Ⓐ traits   Ⓒ trayts
    Ⓑ trates   Ⓓ triats

Post-test

Part 1: Meaning

For each item below, fill in the letter next to the word or phrase that most nearly expresses the meaning of the first word.

> **Sample**
>
> hammer
> (A) part of the arm   (C) a type of vegetable
> ● a tool used for driving nails   (D) to mix thoroughly

1. crucial
(A) silly   (C) important
(B) clear   (D) cruel

2. modify
(A) to change   (C) to place above
(B) to satisfy   (D) to copy

3. fertile
(A) having a bad odor   (C) honorable
(B) annoying   (D) favorable for growing plants

4. potential
(A) strong   (C) invisible
(B) possible   (D) young

5. commitment
(A) a loud speech   (C) the deck of a ship
(B) wreckage   (D) a firm promise

6. exploit
(A) to explain   (C) to exclaim
(B) to take advantage of   (D) to enlarge

7. recuperate
(A) to steal   (C) to recover
(B) to repeat   (D) to go through

8. interval
(A) a signal   (C) a face-to-face meeting
(B) a period of time   (D) a duty

9. decisive
(A) definite   (C) skillful
(B) proper   (D) false

10. influence
(A) to make ill   (C) to make angry
(B) to cause to change   (D) to change the voice

Part 2: Spelling

For each item below, fill in the letter next to the correct spelling of the word.

11. Ⓐ negligance Ⓒ neglagence
    Ⓑ negligence Ⓓ negligense

12. Ⓐ couragous Ⓒ couragus
    Ⓑ curageous Ⓓ courageous

13. Ⓐ achievement Ⓒ achevement
    Ⓑ achievment Ⓓ achevment

14. Ⓐ embarass Ⓒ embarras
    Ⓑ embarrass Ⓓ emberrass

15. Ⓐ stratagy Ⓒ strategy
    Ⓑ stategy Ⓓ stratigy

16. Ⓐ genuine Ⓒ genuien
    Ⓑ genuin Ⓓ genuwine

17. Ⓐ attendence Ⓒ attendance
    Ⓑ atendance Ⓓ attendanse

18. Ⓐ cancelation Ⓒ cancillation
    Ⓑ cancellation Ⓓ cancellasion

19. Ⓐ efficient Ⓒ efficiant
    Ⓑ eficient Ⓓ effishant

20. Ⓐ maintanance Ⓒ maintainence
    Ⓑ maintenence Ⓓ maintenance

21. Ⓐ apearance Ⓒ apearence
    Ⓑ appearance Ⓓ appearence

22. Ⓐ imperal Ⓒ impairal
    Ⓑ imparil Ⓓ imperil

23. Ⓐ convenience Ⓒ convenence
    Ⓑ conveniance Ⓓ convenyence

24. Ⓐ pollitician Ⓒ polatician
    Ⓑ politician Ⓓ politian

25. Ⓐ priorites Ⓒ priorties
    Ⓑ prioraties Ⓓ priorities

26. Ⓐ persue Ⓒ pursue
    Ⓑ persew Ⓓ pursoo

27. Ⓐ confidential Ⓒ confadential
    Ⓑ confidantial Ⓓ confidentiel

28. Ⓐ collegue Ⓒ colleaque
    Ⓑ colleague Ⓓ coleague

29. Ⓐ appropreate Ⓒ appropriet
    Ⓑ aproppriate Ⓓ appropriate

30. Ⓐ satelite Ⓒ satallite
    Ⓑ satellite Ⓓ satalite

STOP

How to Use the Dictionary

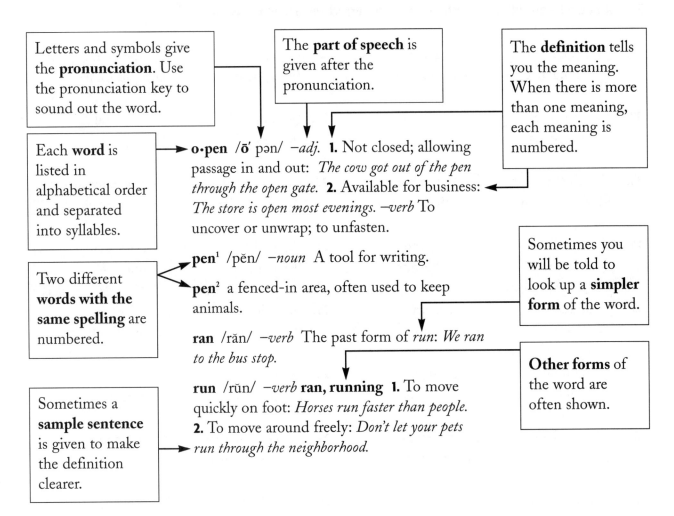

Letters and symbols give the **pronunciation**. Use the pronunciation key to sound out the word.

The **part of speech** is given after the pronunciation.

The **definition** tells you the meaning. When there is more than one meaning, each meaning is numbered.

Each **word** is listed in alphabetical order and separated into syllables.

Two different **words with the same spelling** are numbered.

Sometimes a **sample sentence** is given to make the definition clearer.

Sometimes you will be told to look up a **simpler form** of the word.

Other forms of the word are often shown.

o·pen /ō′ pən/ –*adj.* **1.** Not closed; allowing passage in and out: *The cow got out of the pen through the open gate.* **2.** Available for business: *The store is open most evenings.* –*verb* To uncover or unwrap; to unfasten.

pen[1] /pĕn/ –*noun* A tool for writing.

pen[2] a fenced-in area, often used to keep animals.

ran /răn/ –*verb* The past form of *run*: *We ran to the bus stop.*

run /rŭn/ –*verb* **ran, running** **1.** To move quickly on foot: *Horses run faster than people.* **2.** To move around freely: *Don't let your pets run through the neighborhood.*

Pronunciation Key

ă	cat	ī	ice	ōō	food	hw	which
ā	day	î	near	yōō	cute	zh	usual
â	care	ŏ	hot	ŏŏ	book	ə	about
ä	father	ō	go	ŭ	drum		open
ĕ	wet	ô	law	û	fur		pencil
ē	see	oi	oil	*th*	this		lemon
ĭ	pit	ou	out	th	thin		circus

Mini-Dictionary

a·bun·dant /ə **bŭn′** dənt/ -*adj.* Being in great numbers; more than enough; plentiful: *This year there was abundant rain, so I didn't have to water the garden.*

a·buse /ə **byo͞os′**/ -*noun* **1.** A habit or custom that causes harm: *Drug abuse might cause serious health problems.* **2.** Wrong or improper use; misuse. /ə **byo͞oz′**/ -*verb* **1.** To hurt by treating badly. **2.** Misuse.

ac·cept /ăk **sĕpt′**/ -*verb* **1.** To take or receive: *I accept the birthday gift.* **2.** To regard as true: *Did the teacher accept your answer?*

ac·cess /**ăk′** sĕs/ -*noun* The right or permission to enter or use: *We have access to the building from early in the morning until late at night.*

ac·com·mo·date /ə **kŏm′** ə dāt′/ -*verb* **accommodated, accommodating, accommodates.** To help; provide a service for: *The store was able to accommodate my request.*

ac·com·plish /ə **kŏm′** plĭsh/ -*verb* To carry out; perform: *I have many things I need to accomplish today.*

ac·cu·mu·late /ə **kyo͞om′** yə lāt′/ -*verb* **accumulated, accumulating, accumulates.** To collect; gather; pile up: *Old newspapers can accumulate quickly if they aren't recycled or thrown away.*

ac·cu·rate /**ăk′** yər ĭt/ -*adj.* Exact; free from errors or mistakes; correct: *We need an accurate estimate of how many people will attend the meeting so that we have enough chairs.*

a·chieve·ment /ə **chēv′** mənt/ -*noun* A remarkable act done successfully, especially with great or unusual effort or skill: *Staying in space for six months was a great achievement for the astronaut.*

ac·quire /ə **kwīr′**/ -*verb* **acquired, acquiring, acquires.** To get; obtain; gain: *I want to acquire the ability to use a computer, so I have to take a class.*

a·dapt /ə **dăpt′**/ -*verb* To change to meet new requirements or situations: *When the seasons change, I have difficulty adapting to the different weather.*

ad·dress /ə **drĕs′**/ -*verb* **1.** To deal with directly: *The purpose of the meeting is to address the needs of the neighborhood.* **2.** To speak to.

a·dept /ə **dĕpt′**/ -*adj.* Very skillful; expert: *Betsy is an adept artist.*

ad·e·quate /**ăd′** ĭ kwĭt/ -*adj.* Enough to meet a need for a particular purpose: *The supplies were adequate for a week's camping trip.*

ad·just·a·ble /ə **jŭst′** ə bəl/ -*adj.* Changeable: *The curtains are adjustable to fit windows of any size.*

ad·min·is·ter /ăd **mĭn′** ĭ stər/ -*verb* To direct; manage: *The apartment manager will administer the collection of the rent.*

ad·van·tage /ăd **văn′** tĭj/ -*noun* Something that is useful or helpful; benefit: *Being close to nature is an advantage to living in the country.*

ad·vi·sor /ăd **vī′** zər/ -*noun* **1.** A teacher who helps students select courses and choose a career. **2.** A person who gives advice.

aisle /īl/ -noun A passageway for walking between counters in a store or rows of seats, or a similar place: *I found oatmeal in the cereal aisle.*

al·ter·nate /ôl′ tər nĭt/ -verb **alternated, alternating, alternates.** To happen or follow in turns. -adj. **1.** In place of another: *The road was closed, so we took an alternate route.* **2.** Every other: *The class met on alternate days.*

am·a·teur /ăm′ ə tûr′/ or /ăm′ ə chŏŏr′/ or /ăm′ ə tyŏŏr′/ -noun A person who does something for pleasure rather than money: *The excellent golfer was an amateur who played every day.* -adj. Of or relating to an amateur: *She is an amateur tennis player.*

am·ple /ăm′ pəl/ -adj. **ampler, amplest.** More than enough: *The lunch that was served at the wedding was ample for even the hungriest person.*

an·cient /ān′ shənt/ -adj. **1.** Very old: *A major tourist attraction in Egypt are the ancient pyramids.* **2.** Relating to or having to do with times long past.

an·tic·i·pate /ăn tĭs′ ə pāt′/ -verb **anticipated, anticipating, anticipates.** To think of or about ahead of time: *It is fun to anticipate a vacation.*

ap·peal·ing /ə pē′ lĭng/ -adj. Attractive; pleasing to look at; interesting: *The food at the wedding was both appealing and delicious.*

ap·pear·ance /ə pîr′ əns/ -noun **1.** The way a person or something looks: *A neat appearance is important when someone is applying for a job.* **2.** The act of coming into view.

ap·pe·tite /ăp′ ĭ tīt′/ -noun **1.** A desire for food: *After a long day at work, I have a big appetite.* **2.** A desire or craving.

ap·pro·pri·ate /ə prō′ prē ĭt/ -adj. Suitable; proper: *The clothing was appropriate to wear to a job interview.*

ar·ti·fi·cial /är′ tə fĭsh′ əl/ -adj. **1.** Made by humans; not coming from nature: *I used honey in my tea rather than artificial sweetener.* **2.** Not real; pretended: *The actor's tears were artificial.*

as·sis·tant /ə sĭs′ tənt/ -noun A person who helps or gives aid: *A teacher's assistant may work with students who need extra help.*

as·so·ci·ate /ə sō′ shē āt′/ or /ə sō′ sē āt′/ -verb **associated, associating, associates.** To connect in one's mind: *I associate pumpkins with autumn.* /ə sō′ shē ĭt′/ or /ə sō′ sē ĭt′/ -noun A partner in business.

as·sort·ment /ə sôrt′ mənt/ -noun A group of different kinds of things: *The hardware store had an assortment of nails.*

at·ten·dance /ə tĕn′ dəns/ -noun The number of people present: *The attendance at the meeting was higher than expected.*

au·thor·i·ty /ə thôr′ ĭ tē/ or /ə thŏr′ ĭ tē/ plural **authorities.** -noun **1.** The power to make decisions, act, command people, and enforce laws: *The Congress has the authority to make new laws.* **2.** One who has this power, especially a government or government official: *The store owner reported the robbery to the police, the proper authorities.*

au·thor·ize /ô′ thə rīz′/ -verb **authorized, authorizing, authorizes.** To give power or approval to: *The owner of the store will authorize the clerks to mark down all the fall clothes for the sale.*

au·to·bi·og·ra·phy /ô′ tō bī ŏg′ rə fē/ plural **autobiographies.** -noun A story about a person's life written by that person: *Many famous people write their autobiographies.*

a·vail·a·ble /ə vā′ lə bəl/ -*adj*. Possible to be provided or gotten; obtainable: *Tickets for the baseball game are available at the ballpark.*

a·void /ə void′/ -*verb* **1.** To keep away from: *I try to avoid ticks when I am hiking.* **2.** Prevent from happening.

bal·ance /băl′ əns/ -*noun* **1.** The part that is left over: *After I paid the bills, the balance of my bank account was low.* **2.** A state of equality between two forces. -*verb* **balanced, balancing, balances.** To bring into a state of equality.

bi·as /bī′ əs/ -*noun* A strong feeling for or against something without enough reason and that may get in the way of fair judgment: *Joe has a bias against that football team.* -*verb* To influence in an unfair way.

bi·lin·gual /bī lĭng′ gwəl/ -*adj.* Able to speak two languages well: *The visitor from Italy was bilingual.*

bor·row /bŏr′ ō/ -*verb* To get something from someone else with the promise that it will be returned or replaced: *Linda plans to borrow money to buy a car.*

breathe /brēth/ -*verb* **breathed, breathing, breathes.** To take air into the lungs and let it out; inhale and exhale: *Be sure to breathe regularly when exercising.*

bro·chure /brō shoŏr′/ -*noun* A small pamphlet; booklet: *The travel brochure had some interesting facts about the mountains.*

budg·et /bŭj′ ĭt/ -*noun* A plan for spending money: *It is a good idea for a family to have a budget that is followed throughout the year.* -*verb* **budgeted, budgeting, budgets.** To plan in advance how money will be spent.

busi·ness /bĭz′ nĭs/ -*noun* A person or group of people organized for the purpose of earning money: *Ed decided to start a business selling sporting goods.*

cal·cu·late /kăl′ kyə lāt′/ -*verb* **calculated, calculating, calculates.** To figure out by using mathematics: *We need to calculate how much the trip will cost before we go.*

can·cel·la·tion /kăn′ sə lā′ shən/ -*noun* The act of stopping, ending, or doing away with something: *After the concert's cancellation, the box office refunded money to ticket holders.*

clar·i·fy /klăr′ ə fī/ -*verb* **clarified, clarifying, clarifies.** To make easier to understand: *I need to clarify these instructions so that I can do what you want.*

clev·er /klĕv′ ər/ -*adj.* **cleverer, cleverest.** **1.** Smart; bright; creative: *The clever mechanic repaired the old car.* **2.** Showing mental brightness or creativity: *The clever plan saved the movie hero from disaster.*

col·league /kŏl′ ēg′/ -*noun* A fellow worker; co-worker; associate: *James and his colleague attended the sales meeting.*

col·umn /kŏl′ əm/ -*noun* **1.** A vertical arrangement of items on a page. **2.** A slender upright structure that is used as a support or decoration for a building.

com·mem·o·rate /kə mĕm′ ə rāt′/ -*verb* **commemorated, commemorating, commemorates.** To honor the memory of: *The flags on the graves commemorate those who fought and died for their country.*

com·mence /kə mĕns′/ -*verb* **commenced, commencing, commences.** To begin; start: *The class will commence at 11:00 A.M.*

com·mit·ment /kə **mĭt′** mənt/ –*noun* A strong feeling of being determined to follow a course of action or another person: *Mark made a commitment to finish the computer class.*

com·pel·ling /kəm **pĕl′** ĭng/ –*adj.* Strong; powerful; forceful: *A funeral for a close family member is a compelling reason to take time off from work.*

com·pe·tent /**kŏm′** pĭ tənt/ –*adj.* Able to do something with enough skill or ability; capable: *Because the painters were competent, they finished the job in three days.*

com·pet·i·tive /kəm **pĕt′** ĭ tĭv/ –*adj.* Able to keep up with others in a test of skill or ability: *The baseball player decided to retire at forty-three because he felt he was no longer competitive.*

com·plex /kəm **plĕks′**/ or /**kŏm′** plĕks′/ –*adj.* **1.** Hard to understand: *The complex mathematical problem took hours to solve.* **2.** Made up of many connected or related parts.

com·pli·cat·ed /**kŏm′** plĭ kā′ tĭd/ –*adj.* **1.** Containing many confusing parts: *Computers seem like complicated machines.* **2.** Hard to understand or do.

com·pli·ment /**kŏm′** plə mənt/ –*verb* To praise: *The manager will compliment you on a job well done.* –*noun* An expression of praise.

con·cede /kən **sēd′**/ –*verb* **conceded, conceding, concedes.** To admit as true, often without wanting to: *Sometimes the loser in an election will not concede defeat until the votes have been counted twice.*

con·cep·tion /kən **sĕp′** shən/ –*noun* **1.** The initial formation of a cell in the womb that is capable of developing into a baby. **2.** An idea.

con·cur /kən **kûr′**/ –*verb* **concurred, concurring, concurs.** To have the same opinion; agree: *Parents often concur on major issues involving their children.*

con·dense /kən **dĕns′**/ –*verb* **condensed, condensing, condenses.** To make shorter and to the point: *The newspaper may condense a long story into a few paragraphs.*

con·fi·dence /**kŏn′** fĭ dəns/ –*noun* A strong feeling of being sure of one's ability: *My confidence grew as I practiced my speech over and over.*

con·fi·den·tial /kŏn′ fĭ **dĕn′** shəl/ –*adj.* Told or kept in secret; personal: *A patient's medical records are confidential.*

con·sen·sus /kən **sĕn′** səs/ –*noun* A general agreement or opinion: *The members of the club reached a consensus about the annual fundraiser.*

con·sis·tent /kən **sĭs′** tənt/ –*adj.* Keeping the same actions or ideas: *The teacher's grading scale is consistent from year to year.*

con·ven·ience /kən **vēn′** yəns/ –*noun* The quality of being suitable to one's purposes, comfort, or needs; handy: *Fast-food restaurants are built along busy highways for the convenience of travelers.*

co·op·er·ate /kō **ŏp′** ə rāt′/ –*verb* **cooperated, cooperating, cooperates.** To work or act with others for a common goal: *Football team members must cooperate to win games.*

cou·ra·geous /kə **rā′** jəs/ –*adj.* Having or showing bravery: *The courageous firefighter was honored for saving the lives of three children.*

crave /krāv/ –*verb* **craved, craving, craves.** To desire very much: *Some people crave sweet desserts.*

cri·sis /**krī**′ sĭs/ plural **crises** /**krī**′ sēz/. -*noun* A time of great danger or difficulty: *The earthquake caused a crisis because many roads were damaged or destroyed.*

cri·te·ri·a /krī **tîr**′ ē ə/ plural of **criterion.** *The criteria for people applying for the job were listed in the newspaper.*

cri·te·ri·on /krī **tîr**′ ē ən/ plural **criteria.** -*noun* A rule, standard, or test by which something can be judged.

cru·cial /**kroo**′ shəl/ -*adj.* Of great importance: *It is crucial to be on time for a job interview.*

deb·it /**dĕb**′ ĭt/ -*verb* To charge or subtract from: *When the bank debits my checking account, I must remember to subtract the amount in my checkbook.* -*noun* The charge or subtraction entered in an account.

de·ci·sive /dĭ **sī**′ sĭv/ -*adj.* Firm and beyond doubt: *With sixty-one percent of the voters supporting her, the candidate won a decisive victory in the mayoral race.*

de·duct /dĭ **dŭkt**′/ -*verb* To subtract or take away from: *The bank will deduct the amount of the down payment to get the final amount owed on a house's mortgage.*

de·fi·cien·cy /dĭ **fĭsh**′ ən sē/ plural **deficiencies.** -*noun* A defect or fault; lacking something needed: *There was a vitamin deficiency in the young child's diet because he wouldn't eat vegetables.*

del·e·gate /**dĕl**′ ĭ gāt′/ or /**dĕl**′ ĭ gĭt′/ -*noun* A person or group of persons chosen to speak or act for another or others: *The delegate voted as we asked her to vote.* -*verb* **delegated, delegating, delegates.** To entrust a task to another.

de·pend·ent /dĭ **pĕn**′ dənt/ -*noun* A person who relies on another for support and help: *It is important to claim each dependent when you do your taxes.* -*adj* **1.** Possible, but tied to other conditions. **2.** Requiring the help of another for support.

de·vice /dĭ **vīs**′/ -*noun* Something such as a machine or gadget made for a particular purpose: *An electric hand mixer is a convenient device to have in the kitchen.*

di·a·gram /**dī**′ ə grăm′/ -*noun* A drawing, chart, or figure that shows how something works: *When I saw a diagram of the machine, I understood how it worked.* -*verb* **diagrammed, diagramming, diagrams.** or **diagramed, diagraming, diagrams.** To show by using a diagram.

di·et /**dī**′ ĭt/ -*noun* **1.** The food and drink one usually eats: *Rick kept a record of his diet for a week.* **2.** A special selection of food and drink eaten, especially to improve health or lose or gain weight. -*verb* To eat and drink a certain amount so as to lose weight or control a medical problem.

di·lem·ma /dĭ **lĕm**′ ə/ -*noun* A situation that requires a choice between two things that often seem equally unsatisfactory: *Choosing a candidate for the office was a dilemma.*

dis·a·bil·i·ty /dĭs′ ə **bĭl**′ ĭ tē/ plural **disabilities.** -*noun* The condition of being weakened or unable to do certain physical activities: *His disability made it impossible for him to climb stairs.*

dis·as·ter /dĭ **zăs**′ tər/ -*noun* Something that causes great damage, suffering, distress, or loss: *The flood was a disaster for people living close to the river.*

dis·ci·pline /dĭs′ ə plĭn/ –*noun* **1.** The ability to use self-control: *Following a healthy diet requires discipline.* **2.** Punishment used to correct or train. –*verb* **disciplined, disciplining, disciplines. 1.** To train for the purpose of self control. **2.** To punish someone who needs correcting or training.

dis·close /dĭ sklōz′/ –*verb* **disclosed, disclosing, discloses.** To make known; reveal: *The mayor will disclose the appointments to city offices today.*

dis·crim·i·nate /dĭ skrĭm′ ə nāt′/ –*verb* **discriminated, discriminating, discriminates. 1.** To notice or tell a clear difference: *Sometimes it is hard to discriminate between good and bad computers just by looking at them.* **2.** To treat some people better than others without a good reason or with an unfair reason.

dis·ease /dĭ zēz′/ –*noun* A condition that keeps the body from functioning properly; sickness: *To cure the disease, I had to get a shot.*

dis·sat·is·fied /dĭs săt′ ĭs fīd′/ –*adj.* Displeased with: *Keisha was dissatisfied with the repair work done on her car, so she took it back to the mechanic.*

dis·sim·i·lar /dĭ sĭm′ ə lər/ –*adj.* Not alike; different: *My sister and I are dissimilar in many ways.*

dis·tin·guish /dĭ stĭng′ gwĭsh/ –*verb* To recognize or show as being different: *A hiker should be able to distinguish between poisonous and nonpoisonous snakes.*

dis·tract /dĭ străkt′/ –*verb* To draw away the focus of attention: *I let the loud music distract me from my homework.*

di·ver·sion /dĭ vûr′ zhən/ or /dī vûr′ zhən/ –*noun* Something that changes the attention: *Taking a walk is a good diversion from daily tasks.*

di·ver·si·ty /dĭ vûr′ sĭ tē/ or /dī vûr′ sĭ tē/ plural **diversities.** –*noun* Variety: *The United States is known for its diversity of people.*

di·vulge /dĭ vŭlj′/ –*verb* **divulged, divulging, divulges.** To make known: *People should be careful to whom they divulge their credit card numbers.*

down·size /doun′ sīz′/ –*verb* **downsized, downsizing, downsizes.** To make something smaller: *Debra lost her job when the company downsized her department.*

du·pli·cate /dōō′ plĭ kĭt/ or /dyōō plĭ kĭt/ –*adj.* Exactly like something else: *We gave a duplicate key to the neighbor.* –*noun* A copy or double. –*verb* **duplicated, duplicating, duplicates.** To make a copy or double.

ef·fi·cient /ĭ fĭsh′ ənt/ –*adj.* Bringing about or producing the desired effect with little wasted time, effort, expense, or materials: *Bob is an efficient carpenter.*

e·lim·i·nate /ĭ lĭm′ ə nāt′/ –*verb* **eliminated, eliminating, eliminates.** To do away with; get rid of; remove: *During spring cleaning we try to eliminate all clutter from the house.*

em·bar·rass /ĕm băr′ əs/ –*verb* To make to feel self-conscious, uncomfortable, or ashamed: *Laughing at someone when she makes a mistake might embarrass her.*

en·a·ble /ĕ nā′ bəl/ –*verb* **enabled, enabling, enables.** To give enough power, ability, strength, or opportunity to do something: *Practicing the music will enable me to play the violin at the concert.*

en·coun·ter /ĕn koun′ tər/ –*verb* To meet: *Call for help when you encounter difficulty fixing the roof.* –*noun* An unexpected meeting.

en·cour·age /ĕn **kûr′** ĭj/ or /ĕn **kŭr′** ĭj/ –*verb* **encouraged, encouraging, encourages.** To give hope, confidence, or support to: *A coach tries to encourage the players on the team to play well.*

en·roll /ĕn **rōl′**/ –*verb* To enter into or become a member of something: *I want to enroll in a gardening class.*

ep·i·sode /**ĕp′** ĭ sōd′/ –*noun* An event or incident that is one part of a larger story or time period: *The episode about the storm on the ocean was my favorite part of the book.*

es·sen·tial /ĭ **sĕn′** shəl/ –*adj.* Very important; necessary: *Eating the right food is essential for good health.*

es·ti·mate /**ĕs′** tə māt′/ –*verb* **estimated, estimating, estimates.** To guess about; calculate. /**ĕs′** tə mĭt/ –*noun* A rough guess, calculation, or opinion as of the value, cost, size, or quality of something: *The mechanic gave us an estimate of the cost of the repair work on the car.*

e·val·u·ate /ĭ **văl′** yŏŏ āt′/ –*verb* **evaluated, evaluating, evaluates.** To examine, judge, find out, or estimate the importance or value of: *Before we move to a new city, we must evaluate how the move will affect our lives.*

ev·i·dent /**ĕv′** ĭ dənt/ –*adj.* Easily seen or understood; obvious: *The answer to the question was evident.*

ex·ces·sive /ĭk **sĕs′** ĭv/ –*adj.* More than is necessary, usual, reasonable, or proper: *The truck's price was excessive.*

ex·cur·sion /ĭk **skûr′** zhən/ –*noun* A short pleasure trip; an outing: *Our excursion to the zoo was great fun.*

ex·empt /ĭg **zĕmpt′**/ –*verb* To excuse from a requirement, rule, or duty: *The judge would not exempt the juror because of his age.*

ex·er·cise /**ĕk′** sər sīz′/ –*verb* **exercised, exercising, exercises.** To do physical activity to improve or strengthen the body. –*noun* Physical activity that improves or strengthens the body: *The quarterback did an exercise to strengthen his throwing arm.*

ex·pe·di·tion /**ĕk′** spĭ **dĭsh′** ən/ –*noun* **1.** A trip made for a definite purpose: *The expedition to the North Pole was very dangerous.* **2.** The people making such a trip.

ex·pense /ĭk **spĕns′**/ –*noun* The cost or charge to do or buy something: *The expense of owning a dog includes food and yearly shots.*

ex·ploit /ĭk **sploit′**/ or /**ĕk′** sploit′/ –*verb* **1.** To take advantage of or use unfairly for selfish reasons: *Dishonest salespeople may try to exploit consumers.* **2.** To make practical use of. –*noun* A brave deed or act.

ex·pose /ĭk **spōz′**/ –*verb* **exposed, exposing, exposes. 1.** To leave open to some influence or place in contact with something. **2.** To make known; reveal.

ex·posed past tense of **expose**: *The child was exposed to the cold at nursery school, where another child had one.*

fa·cil·i·ty /fə **sĭl′** ĭ tē/ plural **facilities.** –*noun* Something that provides a service or saves time or effort: *Some hotel rooms have cooking facilities.*

fas·ci·nate /**făs′** ə nāt′/ –*verb* **fascinated, fascinating, fascinates.** To capture and hold interest and attention of: *The white alligator was able to fascinate the people who saw it.*

fa·tigue /fə **tēg′**/ –*noun* Tiredness resulting from hard work or great effort: *The mountain climber felt fatigue after a long climb.* –*verb* **fatigued, fatiguing, fatigues.** To become tired as a result of such effort.

fer·tile /**fûr′** tl/ -*adj.* Good for growing plants and crops: *The farmer was lucky to have such fertile land on his farm.*

fic·tion /**fĭk′** shən/ -*noun* A story that is imaginary or made-up: *I like to read fiction rather than true stories.*

flex·i·ble /**flĕk′** sə bəl/ -*adj.* Able to bend, adjust, or change easily: *The boss asked her workers to learn how to run several machines so that they could be flexible employees.*

fore·cast /**fôr′** kăst′/ -*verb* Tell ahead of time what will happen, especially weather: *Some people say they can forecast rain by looking at the clouds.* -*noun* A prediction.

fright·en·ing /**frīt′** n ĭng/ -*adj.* Causing fear; alarming: *Being caught in a flood is frightening.*

frus·tra·tion /frŭ **strā′** shən/ -*noun* The feeling of being helpless, puzzled, or discouraged: *The girl's frustration at losing the race was great because she had trained for so long.*

gauge /gāj/ -*verb* **gauged, gauging, gauges.** To measure exactly: *Race car drivers must gauge how much fuel they need to finish a race.* -*noun* A standard measure or scale of measurement.

gen·er·ate /**jĕn′** ə rāt′/ -*verb* **generated, generating, generates.** To cause to be; to bring about; produce: *A discussion may generate new ideas.*

gen·u·ine /**jĕn′** yōō ĭn/ -*adj.* **1.** Sincere; honest: *When Pat saw her old friend, her joy was genuine.* **2.** Real; not false: *The diamond is genuine.*

guar·an·tee /găr′ ən **tē′**/ -*verb* **guaranteed, guaranteeing, guarantees.** To promise. -*noun* A promise that something will work or will be repaired or replaced if something goes wrong with it: *The guarantee on the television was for one year.*

guard·i·an /**gär′** dē ən/ -*noun* A person who cares for, protects, or watches over another person: *The children's grandmother was their guardian while their mother was ill.*

head·ache /**hĕd′** āk′/ -*noun* **1.** A pain in the head: *I get a headache if I read in a moving car.* **2.** Something that causes trouble or worry.

head·aches plural of **headache**: *You should see a doctor if you keep getting lots of headaches.*

he·red·i·ty /hə **rĕd′** ĭ tē/ plural **heredities.** -*noun* The characteristics or traits that are passed from parents to their children by genes: *Heredity is responsible for the color of one's eyes and natural hair color.*

hin·der /**hĭn′** dər/ -*verb* To make difficult, get in the way of, or slow progress or movement: *Heavy traffic on the freeway could hinder the drive home from work.*

hon·or /**ŏn′** ər/ -*verb* To show respect or regard for; stand by something: *The voters hoped that the President would honor his promise of a tax cut.* -*noun* **1.** Special respect. **2.** A sense of what is right.

hur·ri·cane /**hûr′** ĭ kān′/ or /**hŭr′** ĭ kān′/ -*noun* A powerful tropical storm.

hy·giene /**hī′** jēn′/ -*noun* Practices, such as cleanliness, that promote good health: *Good hygiene is often taught in health classes.*

im·i·tate /ĭm′ ĭ tāt′/ -*verb* **imitated, imitating, imitates. 1.** To follow the example of: *People often try to imitate others who are successful.* **2.** To copy the behavior or actions of someone else: *My little brother likes to imitate the way I talk.*

im·me·di·ate /ĭ mē′ dē ĭt/ -*adj.* Happening right away, without delay, or very soon: *The doctor said the broken ankle would need immediate attention.*

im·mune /ĭ myoon′/ -*adj.* Protected from a disease either naturally, by a vaccination, or by an injection: *Babies are given shots so that they will be immune to certain diseases.*

im·par·tial /ĭm pär′ shəl/ -*adj.* Not favoring one side over another; fair: *The people judging the debate were impartial.*

im·per·il /ĭm pĕr′ əl/ -*verb* To put in danger: *Driving too fast can imperil you and other drivers on the road.*

im·ple·ment /ĭm′ plə mənt/ -*verb* To put into action or effect; carry out: *The city will implement new rules for trash collection.*

im·pres·sion /ĭm prĕsh′ ən/ -*noun* **1.** A belief, notion, or feeling: *I had the impression that she did not agree with me.* **2.** An effect or feeling that remains on the mind.

im·prop·er /ĭm prŏp′ ər/ -*adj.* Not right; not correct: *The improper electrical wiring in the house caused a fire.*

in·cur /ĭn kûr′/ -*verb* **incurred, incurring, incurs.** To get or come into something by one's own actions: *We incur quite a few expenses throughout the year.*

in·di·cate /ĭn′ dĭ kāt′/ -*verb* **indicated, indicating, indicates. 1.** To be a sign of; show: *Her smile indicates that something good has happened to her.* **2.** To point out: *The map of the city indicates the points of interest.*

in·flu·ence /ĭn′ floo əns/ -*verb* **influenced, influencing, influences.** To cause or affect a change in thought or behavior: *Teachers often are able to influence students to read good books.* -*noun* A person of power affecting another person, thing, or course of events.

in·fre·quent /ĭn frē′ kwənt/ -*adj.* Not happening often; rare: *A total eclipse of the sun is infrequent.*

in·hab·i·tant /ĭn hăb′ ĭ tənt/ -*noun* A person who lives in a certain place: *The inhabitants of Alaska know how to dress for cold weather.*

in·hib·it /ĭn hĭb′ ĭt/ -*verb* To hold back; restrain: *Shyness may inhibit people from meeting new people.*

in·i·tial /ĭ nĭsh′ əl/ -*adj.* Occurring at the beginning; first: *When Tony was late, Dan's initial idea was to not wait for him.*

in·ju·ry /ĭn′ jə rē/ plural **injuries.** -*noun* Damage or harm done to a person or thing: *The ice skater could not compete because of an injury to her leg.*

in·quir·y /ĭn kwīr′ ē/ or /ĭn′ kwə rē/ plural **inquiries.** -*noun* A question: *I made an inquiry about the cost of a round-trip ticket from St. Louis to Boston.*

in·spire /ĭn spīr′/ -*verb* **inspired, inspiring, inspires.** To move, influence, or force to action: *The beautiful sunset inspired Jeff to write a poem about it.*

in·struc·tion /ĭn **strŭk**′ shən/ -*noun*
1. Teaching something to another person:
His instruction on the use of the computer was
very helpful. **2.** Something that is taught.

in·sur·ance /ĭn **shoor**′ əns/ -*noun* Protection
from loss provided by a company in return
for regular payments of a certain amount of
money: *Some states require car owners to have*
automobile insurance in order to get licenses for
their cars.

in·ter·fere /ĭn tər **fîr**′/ -*verb* **interfered,**
interfering, interferes. To get or be in the
way of something: *It is best not to interfere*
in your friends' lives.

in·ter·pret /ĭn **tûr**′ prĭt/ -*verb* **1.** To
understand in a certain way: *Can you interpret*
body language when a person is talking to you?
2. To explain or make clear the meaning of.

in·ter·val /ĭn′ tər vəl/ plural **intervals.**
-*noun* **1.** The space between two places,
points, or objects. **2.** The period of time
between two events.

in·ves·ti·gate /ĭn **vĕs**′ tĭ gāt′/ -*verb*
investigated, investigating, investigates.
To look into carefully to get information or
facts: *Because so many computers are available, you*
should investigate which one will fit your needs.

is·sue /ĭsh′ o͞o/ -*noun* **1.** A subject being
discussed or argued: *Tax relief is one issue*
that the candidates are discussing this year.
2. One copy of a magazine or other periodical.
-*verb* **issued, issuing, issues.** To distribute
for an official reason.

i·tem·ized /ī′ tə mīzd′/ -*adj.* Including or
listing every part or detail: *The mechanic gave*
us an itemized bill for all the repair work done
on the car.

jus·ti·fy /jŭs′ tə fī′/ -*verb* **justified,**
justifying, justifies. 1. To show to be
sensible or reasonable: *Gary was able to*
justify the purchase of a new truck for his
business. **2.** To show to be right or just.

kin·der·gar·ten /kĭn′ dər gär′ tn/ -*noun*
A class for children from four to six years of
age that prepares them for elementary school.

lab·o·ra·to·ry /lăb′ rə tôr′ ē/ plural
laboratories. -*noun* A place with special
equipment for doing scientific tests and
experiments: *The laboratory is testing a new cure*
for the disease.

li·bel /lī′ bəl/ -*noun* The crime of unfairly
damaging a person's good name in written
or printed information: *A newspaper has to*
be careful not to commit libel when it is reporting
a story about someone.

lit·er·a·ture /lĭt′ ər ə cho͝or′/ or /lĭt′ ər ə chər/
-*noun* Writings that have lasting and artistic
value: *Literature is read over and over because*
people can relate to many of the characters.

log·i·cal /lŏj′ ĭ kəl/ -*adj.* Using or agreeing
with the rules of sound reasoning: *The scientist*
presented a logical explanation for the change
of seasons.

lux·u·ry /lŭg′ zhə rē/ or /lŭk′ shə rē/ plural
luxuries. -*noun* Something that is not really
needed but gives enjoyment, pleasure, or
comfort: *A television with a fifty-two-inch*
screen is considered a luxury by most people.

mag·a·zine /măg′ ə zēn′/ or /măg′ ə zēn′/
-*noun* Reading material that is usually issued
weekly or monthly that often contains
articles, stories, pictures, and advertising.

main·te·nance /mān′ tə nəns/ -*noun*
The work of keeping in running condition;
upkeep: *It is important to do regular*
maintenance on a car.

ma·jor·i·ty /mə **jôr′** ĭ tē/ or /mə **jŏr′** ĭ tē/ plural **majorities.** -noun More than half; the greater number of a whole: *The majority of people at the football game wanted the home team to win.*

man·u·al /**măn′** yŏŏ əl/ -adj. Requiring or involving the use of the hands: *Many people like jobs such as woodworking that require manual skills.* -noun. A book that gives instructions.

max·i·mum /**măk′** sə məm/ plural **maximums** or **maxima.** -noun The greatest possible amount, value, or degree. -adj. Being the greatest possible: *The maximum number of movies I may rent at one time is five.*

means /mēns/ -noun The way something is done: *By what means are you going to collect the money for the charity?*

med·i·cine /**mĕd′** ĭ sĭn/ -noun Something that is used to treat a disease or injury: *The doctor said to take the medicine four times a day.*

med·i·cines plural of **medicine**: *Some medicines are better than others for curing certain diseases.*

mo·bil·i·ty /mō **bĭl′** ĭ tē/ -noun The ability to move about: *Once babies can crawl, their mobility increases.*

mod·i·fy /**mŏd′** ə fī/ -verb **modified, modifying, modifies.** To change somewhat; alter: *The pitcher had to modify the throw to the left-handed batter.*

mon·i·tor /**mŏn′** ĭ tər/ -verb To keep watch over; oversee: *Parents should monitor their children's progress in school.*

mo·rale /mə **răl′**/ -noun The attitude, state of mind, or spirit of a person or group: *The morale of the team members was high after they won the playoff game.*

mu·nic·i·pal /myŏŏ **nĭs′** ə pəl/ -adj. Of or relating to a town, city, or other local community or its government: *The municipal elections have several people running for offices.*

mu·se·um /myŏŏ **zē′** əm/ plural **museums.** -noun A building where objects of interest in the fields of art, history, science, or natural history are kept and displayed: *The museum has a collection of paintings by a local artist.*

mys·te·ri·ous /mĭ **stîr′** ē əs/ -adj. Difficult to understand or explain: *The mysterious knocking on the wall scared everyone in the room.*

neg·li·gence /**nĕg′** lĭ jəns/ -noun A failure to do what ought to be done; a failure to use proper care or concern: *My negligence in watering the houseplants caused them to die.*

ne·go·ti·ate /nĭ **gō′** shē āt/ -verb **negotiated, negotiating, negotiates.** To discuss something in order to reach an agreement: *The workers want their union to negotiate a new contract with the company.*

nov·el /**nŏv′** əl/ -noun A fairly long story about made-up characters and events: *The novel was so interesting that I read it all afternoon.*

nu·tri·tion /nŏŏ **trĭsh′** ən/ or /nyŏŏ **trĭsh′** ən/ -noun The process by which a living thing takes in and uses the food that is necessary for life and health: *It is very important for babies to have good nutrition.*

ob·jec·tive /əb **jĕk′** tĭv/ -noun A purpose; goal: *The objective of the article is to inform the reader about the best foods to eat.* -adj. Fair.

ob·sta·cle /**ŏb′** stə kəl/ -noun Something that stands in the way: *Not knowing how to type may be an obstacle to getting a job as a secretary.*

ob·vi·ous /ŏb′ vē əs/ *-adj.* Easily seen or understood: *The answer to the question was obvious after the teacher explained it to me.*

o·mit /ō mĭt′/ *-verb* **omitted, omitting, omits.** To leave out; not include: *The teacher reminded the class to not omit the title on an essay.*

op·tion /ŏp′ shən/ *-noun* A choice: *Sam's option for dinner was to order a pizza.*

o·ral /ôr′ əl/ *-adj.* Spoken; not written: *Nicole's oral book report was very interesting.*

or·gan·i·za·tion /ôr′ gə nĭ zā′ shən/ *-noun* A group of people working together for a certain purpose: *Jason belongs to an organization that collects food for the poor.*

o·ver·whelm /ō′ vər hwĕlm′/ or /ō′ vər wĕlm′/ *-verb* To get the better of: *If you don't keep up with your work, soon it will overwhelm you.*

par·al·lel /păr′ ə lĕl′/ *-adj.* **1.** Alike in many ways; similar: *My friend and I have parallel interests in music and art.* **2.** Extending in the same direction, always the same distance apart, and not meeting.

pas·time /păs′ tīm′/ *-noun* Something that makes free time pass pleasantly: *Our favorite pastime is to go for a long walk in the park.*

pa·tience /pā′ shəns/ *-noun* The ability to put up with trouble, hardship, annoyance, or delay calmly and for a long period of time: *Patience is a good quality for a teacher to have.*

per·ceive /pər sēv′/ *-verb* **perceived, perceiving, perceives. 1.** To become aware of something through sight, hearing, touch, smell, or taste: *After the storm we could perceive a drop in the temperature.* **2.** To understand.

per·ju·ry /pûr′ jə rē/ plural **perjuries.** *-noun* The act of not telling the truth in court after promising to do so: *A person might go to jail if found guilty of perjury.*

per·ma·nent /pûr′ mə nənt/ *-adj.* Lasting or intended to last forever: *The stone wall is a permanent addition to the property.*

per·sist /pər sĭst′/ *-verb* To continue to do something in spite of difficulty or being urged not to: *If you persist in bothering others, you will have to leave.*

per·son·al /pûr′ sə nəl/ *-adj.* Relating to or belonging to a particular person; private: *Kelly said the letter was personal, so she would not read it to me.*

per·son·nel /pûr′ sə nĕl′/ *-noun* The group of people working in a particular business, organization, or other place of employment: *The personnel in the company are paid once a month.*

pe·ti·tion /pə tĭsh′ ən/ *-noun* A formal written paper asking for something: *All the neighbors signed a petition asking for a stop sign to be put at the corner.* *-verb* To make a formal request, especially using a petition.

phys·i·cal /fĭz′ ĭ kəl/ *-adj.* Of or relating to the body: *Walking is a good physical activity.*

phy·si·cian /fĭ zĭsh′ ən/ *-noun* A person who has a license to practice medicine; medical doctor: *My physician said I should stay in bed when I had the flu.*

pol·i·cy /pŏl′ ĭ sē/ plural **policies.** *-noun* A general plan of action: *The new policy will increase safety at the airport.*

pol·i·ti·cian /pŏl′ ĭ tĭsh′ ən/ *-noun* A person who is active in politics, especially one who runs for or holds public office.

pop·u·lar /pŏp′ yə lər/ -adj. Enjoyed or liked by many people: *The popular movie was sold out every night.*

port·a·ble /pôr′ tə bəl/ -adj. Able to be moved or carried easily: *Mike likes to take his portable radio to the baseball game so that he can listen to it while he watches the game.*

pos·i·tive /pŏz′ ĭ tĭv/ -adj. **1.** Favorable. **2.** Having no doubts; sure: *I am positive that tomorrow is my birthday.* **3.** Expressing acceptance: *If your mother's answer is positive, we'll go to the movies.*

po·ten·tial /pə tĕn′ shəl/ -adj. Possible but not yet actual: *Potential voters should find out what the candidates stand for.* -noun Possessing the ability for growth.

pre·cau·tion /prĭ kô′ shən/ -noun An action taken beforehand to avoid a problem, danger, error, or accident: *Wearing a helmet when riding a bicycle is a good safety precaution.*

pre·cise /prĭ sīs′/ -adj. Clearly expressed; exact: *I need precise directions to your house.*

pre·dict /prĭ dĭkt′/ -verb To tell that something is going to happen before it does: *Would you like to be able to predict what you will be doing in ten years?*

pref·er·a·ble /prĕf′ ər ə bəl/ or /prĕf′ rə bəl/ -adj. More desirable: *Which color of paint is preferable to you?*

pres·sure /prĕsh′ ər/ -noun **1.** The act of putting force on something. **2.** The force applied by one thing onto another that it is touching: *The pressure from the weight was uncomfortable.* -verb **pressured, pressuring, pressures.** To use influence to force.

pri·mar·y /prī′ mĕr′ ē/ or /prī′ mə rē/ -adj. Greatest in importance; chief: *Jamal's primary goal is to get an education.*

prin·ci·ple /prĭn′ sə pəl/ -noun A basic belief: *Personal freedom is the main principle for many laws.*

pri·or·i·ties plural of **priority**: *A busy schedule requires that you set priorities to get things done.*

pri·or·i·ty /prī ôr′ ĭ tē/ or /prī ŏr′ ĭ tē/ -noun **1.** Something that is considered more important than other things. **2.** The quality of coming before another in importance or order.

priv·i·lege /prĭv′ ə lĭj/ or /prĭv′ lĭj/ -noun A special right, advantage, or benefit that some people have: *An older child often has the privilege of staying up later than the younger children in a family.*

pro·ce·dure /prə sē′ jər/ -noun A way of doing something or getting something done: *When I got a puppy, I had to learn the procedure for training it.*

pro·claim /prə klām′/ -verb To declare publicly: *The accused man will proclaim his innocence at the trial.*

pro·fes·sion·al /prə fĕsh′ ə nəl/ -adj. **1.** Relating to a profession. **2.** Courteous and businesslike. **3.** Working for money in an activity that other people do as a hobby or for pleasure, such as a sport: *The professional basketball player signed autographs before the game started.*

prov·erb /prŏv′ ûrb/ -noun A short, popular saying that tells a basic truth.

pur·sue /pər sōō′/ -verb **pursued, pursuing, pursues.** To chase after or keep at an activity: *The girl says she will pursue a career as a singer.*

quan·ti·ty /kwŏn′ tĭ tē/ plural **quantities.** -noun The amount or number: *The clerk had to check the quantity of notebooks on the shelf.*

re·al·is·tic /rē′ ə lĭs′ tĭk/ -*adj.* Reasonable and sensible; practical: *Tasha tried to make a realistic schedule of her day's activities.*

re·ceipt /rĕ sēt′/ -*noun* A written statement that says that money has been paid and goods have been received: *To get my money back when I returned the VCR, I had to show my receipt to the clerk.*

re·cent /rē′ sənt/ -*adj.* Happening at a time just before the present: *Recent movies often have many special effects.*

re·cu·per·ate /rĭ kōō′ pə rāt′/ or /rĭ kyōō′ pə rāt′/ -*verb* **recuperated, recuperating, recuperates.** To get back health or strength; recover: *It took six weeks to recuperate from the heart surgery.*

re·deem /rĭ dēm′/ -*verb* **1.** To reform or rescue. **2.** To turn in something, such as a coupon, and get money or goods in exchange: *I will redeem the coupon worth five dollars when I buy the tickets to the soccer game.*

re·duc·tion /rĭ dŭk′ shən/ -*noun* **1.** The act of making something smaller or less: *The reduction of seating space at the theater made it harder to get tickets to the play.* **2.** The amount that something is made smaller or less.

re·lief /rĭ lēf′/ -*noun* **1.** The lessening of pain or distress: *The vacation gave him relief from his stressful job.* **2.** Something that lessens pain or distress.

re·mote /rĭ mōt′/ -*adj.* **remoter, remotest.** Located at a distance; far away: *The plant was from a remote part of the country.*

re·serve /rĭ zûrv′/ -*verb* **reserved, reserving, reserves.** To set aside or save for a particular purpose or person: *If we buy tickets in advance, we can reserve our seats.*

re·side /rĭ zīd′/ -*verb* **resided, residing, resides.** To live in a place; to make one's home: *Some people prefer to reside in the city; some people prefer to reside in the country.*

re·sis·tance /rĭ zĭs′ təns/ -*noun* The ability to reject or withstand the effect of something: *Because I was so tired, my resistance to disease was reduced.*

re·spon·si·ble /rĭ spŏn′ sə bəl/ -*adj.* Accountable for anything that happens or goes wrong: *The person who designed the computer program is responsible for its success.*

re·strict /rĭ strĭkt′/ -*verb* To keep within certain limits: *A snowstorm might restrict airplanes from taking off at the airport.*

route /rōōt/ or /rout/ -*noun* A road, path, or course for traveling from one place to another: *I like to take the shortest route when I go someplace.*

rou·tine /rōō tēn′/ -*noun* A regular way of doing something; standard procedure: *Feeding the dog is part of my morning routine.*

sat·el·lite /săt′ l īt′/ -*noun* **1.** An object placed into orbit to travel around another body in space, such as the earth or moon. **2.** A heavenly body, such as the moon, that travels around a larger body.

sat·is·fac·to·ry /săt′ ĭs făk′ tə rē/ -*adj.* Good enough to meet a need; adequate: *The new television is satisfactory.*

sea·son·al /sē′ zə nəl/ -*adj.* Affected by or coming with one of the four seasons: *Skiing is a seasonal sport.*

sen·ti·ment /sĕn′ tə mənt/ -*noun* **1.** An opinion or point of view: *The present sentiment is that recycling is good for the environment.* **2.** A feeling of emotion.

se·ries /sîr′ ēz/ plural **series.** -*noun* A number of similar things or events coming in a row: *A series of unusual sounds came from the forest.*

se·vere /sə vîr′/ -*adj.* **severer, severest.** Very serious; dangerous: *She suffered from severe pain in her stomach.*

sig·na·ture /sĭg′ nə chər/ -*noun* A person's name written in his or her own handwriting: *A driver's license must have your signature on it.*

sim·pli·fy /sĭm′ plə fī′/ -*verb* **simplified, simplifying, simplifies.** To make simple with fewer parts: *A company that makes VCR's announced that it will simplify the operating instructions.*

soft·ware /sôft′ wâr′/ or /sŏft′ wâr′/ -*noun* Set of instructions that control what a computer does.

so·lu·tion /sə lōō′ shən/ -*noun* An answer to a problem: *The solution to the math problem was easier to find than I thought it would be.*

spouse /spous/ or /spouz/ -*noun* The person one is married to; husband or wife: *My spouse and I have been married for twenty-six years.*

stam·i·na /stăm′ ə nə/ -*noun* The power to keep going while working hard; strength: *The long-distance runner worked hard to increase his stamina.*

strat·e·gy /străt′ ə jē/ plural **strategies.** -*noun* A plan of action: *The coach had decided what would be the best strategy to defeat the other team.*

suc·ceed·ing /sək sēd′ ĭng/ -*adj.* Following in order: *After I translated the first sentence, the succeeding ones were easy to do.*

sur·plus /sûr′ pləs/ or /sûr′ plŭs′/ plural **surpluses.** -*noun* An amount or quantity that is more than what is needed: *When we grow more tomatoes than we need, we give the surplus to a shelter for the homeless.*

sur·vey /sər′ vā′/ or /sûr′ vā′/ -*verb* To look over the parts of: *Before starting a big job, it is a good idea to survey what has to be done.* /sûr′ vā′/ -*noun* An investigation.

sus·pi·cion /sə spĭsh′ ən/ -*noun* The feeling or belief that something is true: *She had a suspicion that her friend was not telling the truth.*

sym·bol /sĭm′ bəl/ -*noun* Something that stands for something else: *One symbol for a country is its flag.*

tech·nique /tĕk nēk′/ -*noun* A method or way a task, especially a difficult or complicated one, is done: *The artist used a rare technique for mixing colors.*

ten·den·cy /tĕn′ dən sē/ plural **tendencies.** -*noun* A likelihood to think or behave a certain way: *Matt has a tendency to look on the bright side of any problem.*

tex·ture /tĕks′ chər/ -*noun* The look and feel of a surface: *The texture of the wool cloth was rough.*

tol·er·ate /tŏl′ ə rāt′/ -*verb* **tolerated, tolerating, tolerates. 1.** To recognize and respect: *Children learn to tolerate the differences in others.* **2.** To put up with.

trait /trāt/ -*noun* A quality that sets one person off from another: *Stacey is known for her trait of having a positive attitude.*

trans·mit /trăns mĭt′/ or /trănz mĭt′/ -*verb* **transmitted, transmitting, transmits.** To send from one place, person, or thing to another: *Do you know how to transmit messages on the computer?*

trans·por·ta·tion /trăns′ pər **tā**′ shən/ –*noun* A way of getting from one place to another: *A school bus is the form of transportation to and from school for many students.*

tra·verse /trə **vûrs**′/ or /**trăv**′ ərs/ –*verb* **traversed, traversing, traverses.** To travel across or pass over: *The hikers will traverse the stony ledge to get to the trail.*

typ·i·cal /**tĭp**′ ĭ kəl/ –*adj.* Showing the special qualities or traits of a group, kind, or type: *A typical puppy is full of energy.*

un·con·ven·tion·al /ŭn′ kən **vĕn**′ shə nəl/ –*adj.* Out of the ordinary: *Pam likes to dress in an unconventional way.*

urge /ûrj/ –*verb* **urged, urging, urges.** **1.** To encourage, persuade, or convince: *The candidate urged the voters to vote for her.* **2.** To force or push on.

ut·most /**ŭt**′ mōst′/ –*adj.* Of the greatest amount: *It is of utmost importance that I finish this job today.*

vague /vāg/ –*adj.* **vaguer, vaguest.** Unclear; not definite: *The governor gave a vague answer to the question about a tax increase.*

val·id /**văl**′ ĭd/ –*adj.* **1.** Acceptable under the law: *The police officer asked to see a valid driver's license.* **2.** Based on facts or evidence.

val·u·a·ble /**văl**′ yōō ə bəl/ or /**văl**′ yə bəl/ –*adj.* **1.** Having great worth, use, or importance: *Old pictures are a valuable way to learn about times past.* **2.** Worth a lot of money.

ver·i·fy /**vĕr**′ ə fī′/ –*verb* **verified, verifying, verifies.** To prove something is true: *Witnesses at the accident will verify how it happened.*

view /vyōō/ –*verb* To look at: *We will view the baby elephant at the zoo.* –*noun* **1.** The act of seeing; sight. **2.** Something that can be seen: *The view of the mountains is beautiful.*

vi·o·late /**vī**′ ə lāt′/ –*verb* **violated, violating, violates.** To break or pay no attention to: *Some drivers violate the speed limit.*

vi·tal /**vīt**′ l/ –*adj.* Very important: *It is vital to turn off the stove when you are finished cooking.*

vo·ca·tion·al /vō **kā**′ shə nəl/ –*adj.* Relating to or providing training in a special skill or trade: *Many students attend a vocational school after high school to learn a trade.*

wage /wāj/ –*noun,* often **wages.** Money paid for work done or services given: *I received the wages for the yard work when I was finished.*

with·draw /wĭ*th* **drô**′/ or /wĭ*th* **drô**′/ –*verb* **withdrew, withdrawn, withdrawing, withdraws.** To take out or away; remove: *I have to withdraw money from the bank before I leave for my vacation.*

Personal Word List

Write any words that need more study. You can write words you see in this book, at work, or at home.

Alphabetical Word List

Word	Lesson	Word	Lesson	Word	Lesson
abundant	20	authorize	1	consistent	23
abuse	5	autobiography	13	convenience	4
accept	3	available	9	cooperate	12
access	14	avoid	1	courageous	20
accommodate	1	balance	1	crave	2
accomplish	23	bias	24	crisis	15
accumulate	2	bilingual	14	criteria	22
accurate	17	borrow	17	crucial	22
achievement	20	breathe	6	debit	1
acquire	7	brochure	7	decisive	19
adapt	9	budget	20	deduct	11
address	9	business	12	deficiency	3
adept	9	calculate	1	delegate	19
adequate	23	cancellation	5	dependent	17
adjustable	1	clarify	23	device	10
administer	11	clever	2	diagram	12
advantage	23	colleague	12	diet	7
advisor	14	column	15	dilemma	22
aisle	4	commemorate	20	disability	11
alternate	10	commence	24	disaster	17
amateur	13	commitment	9	discipline	8
ample	2	compelling	11	disclose	17
ancient	13	competent	9	discriminate	18
anticipate	21	competitive	8	disease	6
appealing	4	complex	17	dissatisfied	5
appearance	7	complicated	10	dissimilar	24
appetite	4	compliment	24	distinguish	23
appropriate	16	concede	19	distract	23
artificial	4	conception	7	diversion	14
assistant	6	concur	19	diversity	18
associate	24	condense	23	divulge	17
assortment	4	confidence	4	downsize	10
attendance	14	confidential	5	duplicate	1
authority	12	consensus	19	efficient	23

Word	Lesson	Word	Lesson	Word	Lesson
eliminate	17	heredity	7	libel	18
embarrass	2	hinder	21	literature	13
enable	19	honor	3	logical	24
encounter	8	hurricane	15	luxury	22
encourage	12	hygiene	7	magazine	13
enroll	14	imitate	21	maintenance	10
episode	13	immediate	7	majority	24
essential	22	immune	8	manual	9
estimate	17	impartial	18	maximum	3
evaluate	24	imperil	15	means	16
evident	23	implement	14	medicine	6
excessive	1	impression	21	mobility	16
excursion	16	improper	2	modify	22
exempt	17	incur	22	monitor	6
exercise	8	indicate	22	morale	12
expedition	20	influence	20	municipal	14
expense	5	infrequent	10	museum	13
exploit	3	inhabitant	20	mysterious	10
exposed	8	inhibit	24	negligence	2
facility	16	initial	24	negotiate	11
fascinate	13	injury	6	novel	13
fatigue	2	inquiry	3	nutrition	4
fertile	20	inspire	21	objective	21
fiction	13	instruction	7	obstacle	16
flexible	10	insurance	5	obvious	3
forecast	15	interfere	18	omit	23
frightening	15	interpret	17	option	11
frustration	9	interval	16	oral	21
gauge	12	investigate	4	organization	15
generate	24	issue	19	overwhelm	22
genuine	21	itemized	5	parallel	15
guarantee	3	justify	22	pastime	13
guardian	8	kindergarten	8	patience	2
headache	6	laboratory	5	perceive	9

Word	Lesson	Word	Lesson	Word	Lesson
perjury	18	reduction	22	transportation	16
permanent	7	relief	7	traverse	20
persist	12	remote	2	typical	11
personal	11	reserve	14	unconventional	24
personnel	5	reside	14	urge	4
petition	19	resistance	8	utmost	20
physical	6	responsible	12	vague	3
physician	6	restrict	5	valid	18
policy	19	route	16	valuable	14
politician	19	routine	8	verify	19
popular	21	satellite	15	view	10
portable	15	satisfactory	3	violate	18
positive	9	seasonal	15	vital	18
potential	19	sentiment	14	vocational	9
precaution	3	series	16	wages	11
precise	1	severe	11	withdraw	1
predict	15	signature	6		
preferable	22	simplify	23		
pressure	6	software	10		
primary	17	solution	12		
principle	18	spouse	1		
priorities	4	stamina	6		
privilege	18	strategy	10		
procedure	11	succeeding	21		
proclaim	18	surplus	2		
professional	8	survey	21		
proverb	13	suspicion	7		
pursue	9	symbol	16		
quantity	12	technique	5		
realistic	11	tendency	8		
receipt	3	texture	4		
recent	16	tolerate	20		
recuperate	5	trait	21		
redeem	2	transmit	10		

Answer Key

Pre-test
Page 10: 1. D, **2.** A, **3.** A, **4.** C, **5.** A, **6.** C, **7.** C, **8.** C, **9.** C, **10.** A
Page 11: 11. C, **12.** A, **13.** A, **14.** D, **15.** B, **16.** C, **17.** D, **18.** B, **19.** A, **20.** B, **21.** D, **22.** A, **23.** C, **24.** B, **25.** D, **26.** C, **27.** B, **28.** A, **29.** D, **30.** C

Unit 1, Lesson 1
Page 13: 1. B, **2.** C, **3.** A, **4.** D, **5.** C, **6.** A, **7.** B, **8.** A, **9.** D, **10.** C, **11.** C, **12.** D
Page 14: 1. accommodate, **2.** precise, spouse; **3.** withdraw, **4.** calculate, **5.** authorize, **6.** adjustable, **7.** avoid, **8.** balance, **9.** calculate, duplicate, accommodate; **10.** excessive, **11–15.** a•void, with•draw, bal•ance, pre•cise, deb•it; **16.** u, s spouse; **17.** d, a, adjustable; **18.** c, s, precise; **19.** c, m, accommodate; **20.** o, i, avoid
Page 15: 1. headache, **2.** carefree, **3.** birthplace, **4.** barefoot, **5.** everlasting, **6.** salesperson, **7.** homemade, **8.** paperback, **9.** haircut, **10.** trustworthy, **11–15.** nowhere, heartbroken, roommate, forehead, teenage
Page 16: debit, avoid, excessive, spouse

Lesson 2
Page 17: 1. B, **2.** D, **3.** B, **4.** B, **5.** C, **6.** D
Page 18: 7. B, **8.** A, **9.** B, **10.** D, **11.** A, **12.** C
Page 19: 1. fatigue, **2.** accumulate, remote, crave; **3.** negligence, patience; **4.** clever, improper; **5.** embarrass, **6.** surplus, **7.** redeem, **8.** ample, **9.** improper, **10.** accumulate, **11–13.** ac•cum•u•late, neg•li•gence, em•bar•rass; **14.** (fatique), fatigue; **15.** (patiance), patience; **16.** (redeam), redeem; **17.** (ampel), ample; **18.** (embarass), embarrass
Page 20: 1. insincere, **2.** immature, **3.** invisible, **4.** impossible, **5.** impolite, **6.** independent, **7.** . . . impatience . . . , **8.** . . . inaccurate . . . , **9.** . . . indirect . . . , **10.** . . . impure . . .
Page 21: redeem, accumulate, embarrass, negligence

Lesson 3
Page 23: 1. B, **2.** D, **3.** B, **4.** A, **5.** C, **6.** A, **7.** C, **8.** B, **9.** A, **10.** D, **11.** B, **12.** A
Page 24: 1. satisfactory, **2.** deficiency, **3.** inquiry, **4.** precaution, **5.** vague, **6.** guarantee, **7.** accept, **8.** receipt, **9.** honor, **10.** exploit, **11–13.** ob•vi•ous, max•i•mum, in•qui•ry; **14.** (vauge), vague; **15.** (deficency), deficiency; **16.** (inquery), inquiry; **17.** (maxamum), maximum; **18.** satisfactory, **19.** accept, **20.** honor
Page 25: 1. accept, **2.** choose, **3.** desert, **4.** already, **5.** lose, **6.** loose, **7.** chose, **8.** dessert
Page 26: choose, obvious, deficiency, precaution, inquiry

Lesson 4
Page 27: 1. B, **2.** C, **3.** B, **4.** A, **5.** D, **6.** D
Page 28: 7. A, **8.** C, **9.** C, **10.** B, **11.** D, **12.** D
Page 29: 1. convenience, **2.** priorities, **3.** aisle, **4.** confidence, convenience; **5.** assortment, appetite, appealing; **6.** artificial, **7.** urge, aisle; **8.** texture, **9.** ti, investigate; **10.** tion, nutrition; **11.** pe, appetite; **12.** peal, appealing; **13.** (nutrishun), nutrition; **14:** (texchur), texture; **15.** (urje), urge
Page 30: 1. busier, **2.** heaviest, **3.** dizziness, **4.** cities, **5.** merciful, **6.** . . . applied . . . , **7.** . . . notified . . . , **8.** . . . hastily . . . , **9.** . . . windiest . . . , **10.** . . . plentiful . . . , **11.** . . . happiness . . . , **12.** . . . lilies . . .
Page 31: appealing, texture, artificial, priorities

Unit 1 Review
Page 32: 1. B. **2.** C, **3.** B, **4.** A, **5.** C, **6.** C, **7.** B, **8.** D, **9.** A, **10.** C
Page 33: 11. B, **12.** C, **13.** A, **14.** D, **15.** D, **16.** C, **17.** D, **18.** A, **19.** A, **20.** B

Unit 2, Lesson 5

Page 35: **1.** C, **2.** D, **3.** A, **4.** C, **5.** A, **6.** B, **7.** D, **8.** A,
9. B, **10.** C, **11.** A, **12.** C

Page 36: **1.** itemized, **2.** personnel, **3.** laboratory,
4. dissatisfied, **5.** insurance, **6.** confidential,
7. technique, **8.** abuse, **9.** restrict, recuperate;
10. abuse, expense; **11.** cancellation, dissatisfied,
personnel; **12.** laboratory, **13.** ized, itemized;
14. lation, cancellation; **15.** ex, expense; **16.** tech,
technique

Page 37: **1.** stopped, **2.** explaining, **3.** confided,
4. insuring, **5.** pleased, **6.** chopping, **7.** . . . restricted . . . ,
8. . . . itemizing . . . , **9.** . . . hopping . . . ,
10. . . . hoping . . . ,

Page 38: personnel, confidential, technique,
dissatisfied

Lesson 6

Page 39: **1.** A, **2.** C, **3.** B, **4.** B, **5.** C, **6.** A

Page 40: **7.** B, **8.** C, **9.** B, **10.** D, **11.** C, **12.** A

Page 41: **1.** physical, physician; **2.** headache,
3. breathe, **4.** pressure, assistant; **5.** injury, **6.** signature,
7. disease, **8.** monitor, **9.** med•i•cine, **10.** stam•i•na,
11. dis•ease, **12.** sig•na•ture, **13.** a, e, breathe; **14.** s, u,
pressure; **15.** c, i, physician; **16.** (headach), headache;
17. (assistent), assistant; **18.** (medacine), medicine

Page 42: **1.** e, **2.** d, **3.** f, **4.** c, **5.** g, **6.** a, **7.** b,
8. . . . MBA . . . , **9.** . . . YMCA . . . , **10.** . . . RBI.

Page 43: stamina, breathe, monitor, injury

Lesson 7

Page 45: **1.** C, **2.** A, **3.** B, **4.** A, **5.** B, **6.** D, **7.** C, **8.** A,
9. A, **10.** B, **11.** B, **12.** D

Page 46: **1.** diet, **2.** relief, hygiene; **3.** permanent,
4. instruction, conception; **5.** hygiene, **6.** appearance,
7. instruction, **8.** suspicion, **9.** brochure,
10. conception, **11.** acquire, **12.** hygiene, immediate;
13. (broshure), brochure; **14.** (appearence),
appearance; **15.** (hygeine), hygiene; **16.** (concepition),
conception

Page 47: **1.** . . . attendance . . . , **2.** . . . election . . . ,
3. . . . action . . . , **4.** . . . assistance . . . , **5.** . . . television.,
6. . . . corrections . . .

Page 48: diet, heredity, permanent, hygiene

Lesson 8

Page 49: **1.** D, **2.** B, **3.** B, **4.** A, **5.** C, **6.** C

Page 50: **7.** B, **8.** D, **9.** B, **10.** C, **11.** A, **12.** B

Page 51: **1.** resistance, **2.** exposed, **3.** competive,
4. professional, **5.** guardian, **6.** discipline, routine;
7. professional, immune; **8.** exposed, exercise;
9. tendency, **10.** kindergarten, **11.** encounter,
12. guardian, **13.** immune, exposed, routine; **14.** tine,
routine; **15.** pline, discipline; **16.** an, guardian

Page 52: Sample answers: **1.** conductor, one who
conducts or leads; **2.** musician, person who plays
music; **3.** librarian, one who runs a library;
4. computer, that which computes or calculates;
5. electrician, one who knows how to work with
electricity; **6.** artist, one who is skillful in art;
7. actor, one who acts; **8.** humidifier, that which
humidifies

Page 53: routine, kindergarten, resistance, exposed

Unit 2 Review

Page 54: **1.** B, **2.** C, **3.** A. **4.** A, **5.** D, **6.** C. **7.** C, **8.** B,
9. D, **10.** A, **11.** D, **12.** A

Page 55: **13.** C, **14.** A, **15.** D, **16.** D, **17.** C, **18.** B, **19.** A,
20. D, **21.** C, **22.** A, **23.** D, **24.** A

Unit 3, Lesson 9

Page 57: **1.** D, **2.** B, **3.** A, **4.** D, **5.** C, **6.** B, **7.** A, **8.** C,
9. D, **10.** A, **11.** C, **12.** B

Page 58: **1.** manual, vocational; **2.** frustration,
3. address, **4.** competent, commitment; **5.** perceive,
6. adapt, adept; **7.** positive, **8.** pursue, **9.** adapt,
10. address, **11.** adept, **12.** available, **13.** a, u, a,
manual; **14.** u, u, e, pursue; **15.** o, e, e, competent;
16. e, e, i, e, perceive; **17.** (committment),

commitment; **18.** (manuel), manual; **19.** (percieve), perceive; **20.** (addres), address

Page 59: Each sentence should begin with a capital letter and end with the punctuation indicated. Individual sentences will vary. Possible answers: **1.** A long line of people waited for the office to open. **2.** Did you see an ad in the newspaper? **3.** I went to a good vocational school. **4.** I got a pay raise! **5.** Where can I find the bulletin board? **6.** Always try to improve your job skills. **7.** Good manual skills can be used in many ways. **8.** Can you get over that feeling of frustration?

Page 60: competent, adept, vocational, positive

Lesson 10

Page 61: **1.** A, **2.** B, **3.** B, **4.** C, **5.** D, **6.** B
Page 62: **7.** C, **8.** B, **9.** D, **10.** D, **11.** B, **12.** A
Page 63: **1.** maintenance, **2.** flexible, **3.** alternate, **4.** mysterious, **5.** software, **6.** downsize, **7.** view, **8.** device, **9.** strategy, **10.** infrequent, **11.** complicated, **12.** mysterious, **13.** maintenance, **14.** device, **15–18.** al•ter•nate, down•size, in•fre•quent, trans•mit
Page 64: **1.** …Coach Johnson., **2.** …Mr. Rogers … Helen Fisher, **3.** …Doctor Potter …, **4.** …Aunt Tanya …, **5.** …Senator Winston Smith., **6.** …Professor Rivera's …, **7.** …Ms. Tina Wing …, **8.** …Reverend Steven Burger
Page 65: maintenance, Mr. Blake, complicated, strategy

Lesson 11

Page 67: **1.** D, **2.** A, **3.** B. **4.** B, **5.** C, **6.** D, **7.** A, **8.** D, **9.** C, **10.** A, **11.** C, **12.** C
Page 68: **1.** disability, **2.** compelling, **3.** procedure, **4.** realistic, **5.** wages, **6.** personal, **7.** typical, **8.** administer, **9.** option, **10.** severe, **11.** option, **12.** deduct, **13.** negotiate, **14.** typical, **15.** realistic, **16.** personal, **17.** (nagotiate), negotiate, **18.** (proceedure), procedure, **19.** (personnal), personal, **20.** (typecal), typical

Page 69: **1.** …United Kingdom …, **2.** …South Side Bowling Club …, **3.** …Fourth of July …, **4.** …Western Driving School? Possible answers: **5.** The New Light Congregation …, **6.** …Dallas, **7.** …the Gold Star Motorcycle Club, **8.** … Hanover Community College
Page 70: procedure, negotiate, realistic, disability

Lesson 12

Page 71: **1.** B, **2.** C, **3.** A, **4.** D, **5.** A, **6.** B
Page 72: **7.** D, **8.** B, **9.** A, **10.** B, **11.** C, **12.** B
Page 73: **1.** gauge, **2.** business, **3.** encourage, **4.** morale, **5.** solution, **6.** persist, **7.** colleague, **8.** quantity, authority; **9.** cooperate, **10.** responsible, **11.** o, o, e, a, e, cooperate; **12.** i, a, a, diagram; **13.** a, u, e, gauge; **14.** a, u, o, i, authority; **15.** o, a, e, morale; **16.** quantity, **17.** persist, **18.** encourage
Page 74: **1.** Ms. Juanita Ruiz, **2.** Lester Waxman, **3.** HH Industries, **4.** Area Supervisor, **5.** CA, **6.** comma, **7.** colon, **8.** comma
Page 75: solution, morale, business, encourage

Unit 3 Review

Page 76: **1.** B, **2.** A, **3.** D, **4.** A, **5.** C, **6.** C, **7.** B, **8.** A, **9.** D, **10.** B, **11.** B, **12.** A
Page 77: **13.** C, **14.** B, **15.** A, **16.** D, **17.** C, **18.** A, **19.** A, **20.** D, **21.** B, **22.** B, **23.** D, **24.** D

Unit 4, Lesson 13

Page 79: **1.** B, **2.** C, **3.** A, **4.** D, **5.** B, **6.** A, **7.** C, **8.** B, **9.** A, **10.** D, **11.** A, **12.** C
Page 80: **1.** novel, **2.** ancient, **3.** pastime, **4.** proverb, **5.** fiction, **6.** episode, **7.** magazine, **8.** autobiography, **9.** proverb, **10.** ancient, **11.** literature, **12.** fascinate, **13.** museum, **14.** amateur, **15.** t, e, pastime; **16.** e, u, amateur; **17.** c, i, fascinate; **18.** o, a, autobiography

Page 81: 1. biology, the study of living things; **2.** phonograph, a device that reproduces sounds; **3.** automobile, a vehicle for transporting one or more people; **4.** telephone, an instrument that transmits sounds at a distance; **5.** microphone, a device used to make sounds louder; **6.** photograph, an image that is made using light; **7.** telegraph, a device for communicating over long distances; **8.** monogram, a letter or letters used to identify someone; **9.** bicycle, a device made with two wheels that is used for transportation; **10.** telescope, an instrument used to look at far-away objects

Page 82: episode, fiction, literature, autobiography

Lesson 14

Page 83: 1. C, **2.** C, **3.** A, **4.** A, **5.** D, **6.** B

Page 84: 7. B, **8.** A, **9.** D, **10.** B, **11.** A, **12.** C

Page 85: 1. implement, sentiment; **2.** bilingual, **3.** reserve, **4.** valuable, **5.** municipal, **6.** attendance, **7.** advisor, **8.** sentiment, **9.** diversion, **10.** reside, **11.** en, enroll; **12.** cess, access; **13.** i, municipal; **14.** a, valuable; **15.** dance, attendance; **16.** di, diversion; **17.** i, sentiment; **18.** sor, advisor

Page 86: 2. …advisor's suggestion…, **3.** …school's classroom…, **4.** …players' sentiment…, **5.** …company's benefits…, **6.** …employees' attendance…, **7.** …manager's explanation…, **8.** …workers' safety…, **9.** …classroom's location…, **10.** …counselors' report…,

Page 87: municipal, access, company's, Attendance

Lesson 15

Page 89: 1. A, **2.** D, **3.** B, **4.** B, **5.** C, **6.** D, **7.** A, **8.** C, **9.** B, **10.** A, **11.** C, **12.** C

Page 90: 1. seasonal, **2.** column, **3.** parallel, satellite; **4.** organization, **5.** hurricane, **6.** frightening, **7.** crisis, frightening, predict; **8.** imperil, **9.** forecast, **10.** portable, **11.** organization **12.** imperil **13.** predict, **14.** column, **15.** satellite, satellite; **16.** huricane, hurricane; **17.** parallell, parallel; **18.** frightaning, frightening

Page 91: 1. plumber, **2.** wrapper, **3.** cupboard, **4.** solemn, **5.** fasten, **6.** hustle, **7.** Autumn, **8.** raspberries, **9.** glisten, **10.** shepherd, **11.** limber, limb; **12.** bombard, bomb; **13.** crumble, crumb; **14.** soft, soften; **15.** moist, moisten; **16.** signal, sign

Page 92: hurricane, parallel, organization, satellite

Lesson 16

Page 93: 1. C, **2.** A, **3.** B, **4.** A, **5.** D, **6.** C

Page 94: 7. C, **8.** C, **9.** A, **10.** B, **11.** B, **12.** C

Page 95: 1–4. in•ter•val, mo•bil•i•ty, ob•sta•cle, sym•bol; **5.** interval, symbol; **6.** recent, **7.** appropriate, **8.** series, means; **9.** mobility, **10.** route, means; **11.** transportation, **12.** interval, **13.** facility, mobility; **14.** symbol, **15.** a, l, obstacle; **16.** p, a, appropriate; **17.** o, e, route; **18.** e, a, interval

Page 96: 1. comic, **2.** guest, **3.** object, **4.** series, **5.** motor, **6.** eight, **7.** ate, **8.** royal, **9.** urban, **10.** jury, **11.** feature, **12.** fiction, **13.** sauce, **14.** ground, **15.** parson

Page 97: transportation, route, interval, facility

Unit 4 Review

Page 98: 1. B, **2.** C, **3.** A, **4.** B, **5.** D, **6.** C, **7.** B, **8.** A, **9.** D, **10.** C, **11.** A, **12.** B

Page 99: 13. B, **14.** A, **15.** C, **16.** D, **17.** B, **18.** B, **19.** D, **20.** C, **21.** A, **22.** D, **23.** B, **24.** B

Unit 5, Lesson 17

Page 101: 1. C, **2.** B, **3.** A, **4.** D, **5.** B, **6.** A, **7.** C, **8.** D, **9.** A, **10.** B, **11.** D, **12.** A

Page 102: 1. complex, **2.** accurate, **3.** exempt, **4.** borrow, accurate; **5.** primary, **6.** disclose, disaster; **7.** disclose, **8.** accurate, estimate, eliminate; **9.** borrow, **10.** mate, estimate; **11.** ex, exempt; **12.** vulge, divulge; **13.** dependant, dependent; **14.** interprat, interpret; **15.** elimanate, eliminate

Page 103: Sentences will vary. **1.** exhale, **2.** exclude, **3.** explode, **4.** export, **5.** exit, **6.** extinguish, **7.** expand, **8.** expire

Page 104: interpret, accurate, exempt, disclose

Lesson 18

Page 105: 1. B, 2. D, 3. A, 4. B, 5. C, 6. C

Page 106: 7. D, 8. B, 9. A, 10. B, 11. A, 12. C

Page 107: 1. impartial, 2. vital, libel; 3. proclaim, 4. diversity, 5. privilege, interfere; 6. violate, 7. perjury, 8. proclaim, privilege, principle; 9. ple, principle; 10. ter, interfere; 11. tal, vital; 12. bel, libel; 13. si, diversity; 14. per, perjury; 15. tial, impartial; 16. in, discriminate

Page 108: 1. . . . capital . . . , 2. . . . principle . . . , 3. . . . whole . . . , 4. . . . buy . . . , 5. . . . sole . . .

Page 109: perjury, principle, impartial, interfere

Lesson 19

Page 111: 1. A, 2. C, 3. D, 4. B, 5. B, 6. D, 7. C, 8. A, 9. C, 10. D, 11. A, 12. C

Page 112: 1. consensus, 2. decisive, 3. issue, 4. enable, 5. verify, 6. politician, 7. concede, concur; 8. delegate, 9–12. petition, policy, politician, potential; 13–15. is•sue, con•cede, con•cur; 16. ti, petition; 17. ci, decisive; 18. cian, politician; 19. sus, consensus; 20. sue, issue

Page 113: Sentences will vary. 1. compile, 2. confer, 3. conjunction, 4. connect, 5. compress, 6. contract, 7. contaminate, 8. connect

Page 114: issue, concede, petition, politician

Lesson 20

Page 115: 1. C, 2. A, 3. D, 4. B, 5. C, 6. C

Page 116: 7. A, 8. B, 9. B, 10. C, 11. D, 12. C

Page 117: 1. traverse, budget, fertile, utmost; 2. achievement, 3. courageous, 4. inhabitant, 5. commemorate, 6. tolerate, commemorate; 7. inhabitant, abundant; 8. expedition, 9. influence, 10. utmost, 11. traverse, 12. achievement, 13. courageous, 14. abundance, 15. tolerate, 16. tile, fertile; 17. pe, expedition; 18. o, commemorate

Page 118: 1. . . . buffalo, geese, and prairie dogs. 2. No commas needed. 3. Sickness, injury, and boredom . . . , 4. . . . narrow, rocky, and dangerous. 5. Go to the store, buy a new cap, and pay for it with a check. 6. . . . cold, sweet, and fresh. 7. . . . across the hall, through the room, and under the rug. 8. No commas needed.

Page 119: abundant, courageous, . . . soldiers, Native Americans, and settlers . . . , influence

Unit 5 Review

Page 120: 1. C, 2. B, 3. A, 4. D, 5. C, 6. A, 7. D, 8. C, 9. A, 10. B, 11. D, 12. C

Page 121: 13. B, 14. A, 15. C, 16. C, 17. A, 18. D, 19. B, 20. A, 21. C, 22. C, 23. D, 24. A

Unit 6, Lesson 21

Page 123: 1. B, 2. A, 3. C, 4. D, 5. D. 6. C, 7. A, 8. C, 9. B, 10. A, 11. C, 12. D

Page 124: 1. inspire, 2. impression, 3. popular, 4. hinder, 5. survey, 6. oral, 7. succeeding, 8. oral, inspire; 9. survey, 10. trait, 11. anticipate, imitate; 12. impression, imitate; 13. an•tic•i•pate, 14. gen•u•ine, 15. ob•jec•tive, 16. ine, genuine, 17. ceed, succeeding; 18. der, hinder

Page 125: 1. exception, 2. contribution, 3. judgment (judgement is also acceptable), 4. arrangement, 5. construction, 6. equipment, 7. . . . encouragement . . . , 8. . . . inspection . . . , 9. . . . dedication . . . , 10. . . . prevention. . .

Page 126: anticipate, succeeding, impression, genuine

Lesson 22

Page 127: 1. C, 2. A, 3. D, 4. C, 5. A, 6. B

Page 128: 7. B, 8. D, 9. B, 10. A, 11. C, 12. B

Page 129: 1. modify, justify; 2. reduction, 3. essential, dilemma; 4. overwhelm, 5. incur, indicate; 6. criteria,

7. crucial, **8.** luxury, **9.** preferable, **10.** essential,
11. reduction, **12.** modify, **13.** criteria, **14.** incur,
15. crucial, **16.** luxury
Page 130: 1. …washable, **2.** …enjoyable…,
3. …passable, **4.** …workable, **5.** …advisable…,
6. …comfortable…, **7.** …usable…, **8.** …acceptable…
Page 131: luxury, incur, preferable, crucial

Lesson 23
Page 133: 1. B, **2.** C, **3.** B, **4.** D, **5.** A, **6.** C, **7.** B, **8.** D,
9. D, **10.** A, **11.** C, **12.** B
Page 134: 1. consistent, efficient, evident;
2. accomplish, efficient; **3.** simplify, clarify;
4. distract, **5.** distinguish, **6.** omit, **7.** advantage,
adequate; **8.** condense, consistent; **9.** adequate,
10. advantage, **11.** accomplish, **12.** distract, **13.** dense,
condense; **14.** guish, distinguish; **15.** fy, clarify;
16. pli, simplify; **17.** i, evident, **18.** mit, omit
Page 135: 1. IL **2.** NH **3.** NV **4.** NC **5.** OH **6.** AL
7. OR **8.** NJ **9.** TX **10.** AZ **11.** AR **12.** MN **13.** CO
14. IA **15.** MA **16.** NE **17.** MS **18.** KS **19.** TN
20. WV **21.** CA **22.** NY **23.** WA **24.** ME
Page 136: evident, accomplish, distract, clarify

Lesson 24
Page 137: 1. A, **2.** D, **3.** C, **4.** B, **5.** B, **6.** C
Page 138: 7. C, **8.** B, **9.** D, **10.** A, **11.** B, **12.** D
Page 139: 1. dissimilar, commence, associate; **2.** bias,
3. logical, **4.** majority, **5.** generate, associate,
evaluate; **6.** inhibit, initial; **7.** dissimilar, **8.** logical,
unconventional, initial; **9.** compliment,
10. commence, compliment; **11.** con, tion,
unconventional; **12.** ity, majority; **13.** gen, ate,
generate; **14.** e, u, evaluate, **15.** as, bias; **16.** hib,
inhibit

Page 140: 1. 395 Oxford Blvd., Bloomington, IL
61701, **2.** 908 Acorn Plz., Haverhill, MA 01832,
3. 12 Spring Gdns. Ave., Waterloo, IA 50722,
4. 4532 Backer Sq., Fresno, CA 93740, **5.** 1936
Five Oaks Dr., Durham, NC 27707, **6.** 328
Biscayne Tr., Seattle, WA 98124, **7.** 932 William
Tell Pkwy., Gulfport, MS 39503, **8.** 1919
Tanglewood Terr., Escondido, CA 92033
Page 141: majority, generate, compliments,
unconventional

Unit 6 Review
Page 142: 1. C, **2.** D, **3.** A, **4.** B, **5.** C, **6.** B, **7.** B, **8.** D,
9. A, **10.** D, **11.** C, **12.** B
Page 143: 13. C, **14.** A, **15.** D, **16.** D, **17.** B, **18.** C,
19. A, **20.** A, **21.** D, **22.** C, **23.** B, **24.** A

Post-test
Page 144: 1. C, **2.** A, **3.** D, **4.** B, **5.** D, **6.** B, **7.** C, **8.** B,
9. A, **10.** B
Page 145: 11. B, **12.** D, **13.** A, **14.** B, **15.** C, **16.** A,
17. C, **18.** B, **19.** A, **20.** D, **21.** B, **22.** D, **23.** A, **24.** B,
25. D, **26.** C, **27.** A, **28.** B, **29.** D, **30.** B

Scoring Chart

Use this chart to find your score. Line up the number of items with the number correct.
For example, if 14 out of 15 items are correct, the score is 93.3 percent.

Number Correct

Number of Items

	5	6	7	8	9	10	11	12	13	14	15	16	17	18	19	20	21	22	23	24	25	26	27	28	29	30
5	100																									
6	83.3	100																								
7	71.4	85.7	100																							
8	62.5	75	87.5	100																						
9	55.5	66.7	77.7	88.9	100																					
10	50	60	70	80	90	100																				
11	45.4	54.5	63.6	72.7	81.8	90.9	100																			
12	41.7	50	58.3	66.7	75	83.3	91.7	100																		
13	38.5	46.1	53.8	61.5	69.2	76.9	84.6	92.3	100																	
14	35.7	42.8	50	57.1	64.3	71.4	78.5	85.7	92.8	100																
15	33.3	40	46.6	53.3	60	66.7	73.3	80	86.7	93.3	100															
16	31.2	37.5	43.7	50	56.2	62.5	68.7	75	81.2	87.5	93.7	100														
17	29.4	35.3	41.2	47	52.9	58.8	64.7	70.6	76.5	82.3	88.2	94.1	100													
18	27.8	33.3	38.9	44.4	50	55.5	61.1	66.7	72.2	77.8	83.3	88.9	94.4	100												
19	26.3	31.6	36.8	42.1	47.4	52.6	57.9	63.1	68.4	73.7	78.9	84.2	89.4	94.7	100											
20	25	30	35	40	45	50	55	60	65	70	75	80	85	90	95	100										
21	23.8	28.6	33.3	38.1	42.8	47.6	52.3	57.1	61.9	66.7	71.4	76.1	80.9	85.7	90.5	95.2	100									
22	22.7	27.3	31.8	36.4	40.9	45.4	50	54.5	59.1	63.6	68.1	72.7	77.2	81.8	86.4	90.9	95.4	100								
23	21.7	26.1	30.4	34.8	39.1	43.5	47.8	52.1	56.5	60.8	65.2	69.5	73.9	78.3	82.6	86.9	91.3	95.6	100							
24	20.8	25	29.2	33.3	37.5	41.7	45.8	50	54.2	58.3	62.5	66.7	70.8	75	79.1	83.3	87.5	91.6	95.8	100						
25	20	24	28	32	36	40	44	48	52	56	60	64	68	72	76	80	84	88	92	96	100					
26	19.2	23.1	26.9	30.8	34.6	38.5	42.3	46.2	50	53.8	57.7	61.5	65.4	69.2	73.1	76.9	80.8	84.6	88.5	92.3	96.2	100				
27	18.5	22.2	25.9	29.6	33.3	37	40.7	44.4	48.1	51.9	55.6	59.2	63	66.7	70.4	74.1	77.8	81.5	85.2	88.9	92.6	96.3	100			
28	17.9	21.4	25	28.6	32.1	35.7	39.3	42.9	46.4	50	53.6	57.1	60.7	64.3	67.9	71.4	75	78.6	82.1	85.7	89.3	92.9	96.4	100		
29	17.2	20.7	24.1	27.6	31	34.5	37.9	41.4	44.8	48.3	51.7	55.2	58.6	62.1	65.5	69	72.4	75.9	79.3	82.8	86.2	89.7	93.1	96.6	100	
30	16.7	20	23.3	26.7	30	33.3	36.7	40	43.3	46.7	50	53.3	56.7	60	63.3	66.7	70	73.3	76.7	80	83.3	86.7	90	93.3	96.7	100